TEACHING DANCE
TO
SENIOR ADULTS

TEACHING DANCE
TO
SENIOR ADULTS

By

LIZ LERMAN

With Forewords by

Anna Halprin

and

Solomon Jacobson, Ph.D.

CHARLES C THOMAS • PUBLISHER
Springfield • Illinois • U.S.A.

Published and Distributed Throughout the World by

CHARLES C THOMAS • PUBLISHER
2600 South First Street
Springfield, Illinois 62717

© *1984 by* CHARLES C THOMAS • PUBLISHER
ISBN 0-398-04903-3 (cloth)
ISBN 0-398-06641-8 (paper)
Library of Congress Catalog Card Number: 83-5115

Printed in the United States of America
Q-R-3

Library of Congress Cataloging in Publication Data

Lerman Liz.
    Teaching dance to senior adults.

    Bibliogrpahy: p.
    Includes index.
    1. Modern dance — Study and teaching.
2. Aged — Recreation. I. Title.
GV1753.5.L47 1984   793.3'2   83-5115
ISBN 0-398-04903-3. —ISBN 0-398-06641-8 (pbk.)

In Memory of
Anne Lerman
and
Jo Apter

I MYSELF am an elder. I'm sixty-three years of age and a lifelong dancer. My greatest dance achievement was healing myself of cancer through dance. I am a cancer survivor and attribute that survival to restoring my body through movement awareness and dance with imagery of positive and life renewing values.

> *Grow young along with me!*
> *The best is yet to come*
> *The last of life, for which*
> *the first was made.*
> Rabbi Ben Ezra

Those whom the gods love grow young. It's true. The gods love those who grow young because they have taken the trouble to do so. The chronologically young is a given gift; growing young into what is called old age is an achievement, a work of art. It is an incredible achievement in our western culture, where the stereotypes are filled with degrading, even contemptible myths. You've heard them:

Old people should be dignified and circumspect.

Old dogs cannot learn new tricks.

Old people are closed minded, set in their ways, slow, and senile.

Old people are ugly.

There is no future for old people, so why teach them?

Old people don't want to touch or use their bodies.

Old people aren't interested in sensual or sexual experiences.

Old people like to sit still and be quiet.

These myths are nightmares. They may indeed be a warning, but they are not inevitable truths. If we are seduced into believing these ideas, they become the very images that form and shape our existence. We all have the potential to be fulfilled and spirited all of our lives. One of my most inspirational and delightful friends is don José, a 107-year-old Huichol Indian medicine man, who leads large groups of people in the sacred deer dance of his tribe.

I am satisfied to be my age and to grow old, but with life-supporting and new, meaningful images of what old means. For me, "growing" old can provide lots more time to have fun, be playful, pay attention to taking care of myself, be with my young family, and above all nourish my spiritual dimension. What is your list? Whatever it is, dance is a marvelous way to fulfill and gratify these desires. The experience of dancing constitutes something more than the body in motion. There is a release and a replenishment of psychic energy that leaves one with an oceanic feeling of freedom, from which all constraint has fallen away.

Not only is dancing constructive and beneficial, it is also uplifting. I can't think of any other activity of greater therapeutic and spiritual value. Perhaps I can best describe what dance can mean to elders by sharing this story. A few years ago I was asked to create a dance for a gerontology conference to be held in San Francisco with an estimated attendance of over 2,000 people. The theme for this conference was "The Celebration of Life." After talking with many elders, one recurrent notion came to the foreground—not wanting to be isolated and wanting instead to be with other people of all ages. With this in mind, I gathered eighty people ranging in age from a six-month-old baby to a ninety-four-year-old man. We held a series of workshops, and together we mutually created a dance. It was a joyous experience to witness the excitement and caring ways with which all the ages shared their unique humanness with one another.

My mother, eighty-nine years of age, and my father, ninety-four years of age, agreed to participate in this dance performance. When I asked my father what was most important to him in life, he answered, "Love." He went on to tell me that it was his love for his wife, Ida. He said he loved all of us, his children, but that he loved Ida with his soul. For weeks before the performance he began to image himself dancing with her. When the performance day arrived, he told me he was going to dance with Ida. My father's legs had given out, and he had been in a wheelchair for three years. But when he wheeled on stage, he managed to get out of his wheelchair, stand up and holler, "Come on, Ida, let's dance." Through the power of imagery and his spirit, my father, for a split second, took my mother in his arms and danced his love dance with Ida. In doing this dance, he fulfilled and achieved the essence of his being. Not even Nureyev could have done a more astonishing and beautiful dance than Isadore and Ida Schuman, age ninety-four and eighty-nine.

Dance is a powerful human force for transforming and living the life we image.

ANNA HALPRIN

FOREWORD

CREATIVITY is often arrested in the aged. It is imprisoned by inhibitions, habits, and expectations. When it is released, we get a Grandma Moses creating vibrant paintings in the primitive style. If it is never inhibited, we have Picasso creating until the week of his death. Creativity can be released in many ways—through poetry, literature, autobiography, crafts, and volunteer or paid work in the helping professions. The experiences and emotions of older persons can be translated into vibrant, creative works. Usually, however, there must be a program and a setting that encourages and channels free expression into an art form.

Consider the dance. Here a person uses his or her body to express a mood or feeling. The body moves in rhythm and pattern that unmistakably differs from our everyday movements. Yet dance is based primarily on the walk. Anyone who can walk can dance. The dance is also based on everyday gestures, such as the wave of a hand, so anyone who can wave can dance. The magic of dances comes in controlling the walk or the wave to create meaning for the dancer and thus the audience watching the dancer.

Create a dance right now. Wave goodbye to someone. They are leaving. Wave slowly and sadly—feel your arm gain weight. Wait! They are returning. Wave them back. Use both hands. There, you have created a dance. If you got up, still waving your hands, perhaps your body swayed in a spontaneous dance of pleasure at a reunion.

Music and dance, I believe, sprang from the internal rhythms of our bodies. If we listen to our own beats, we create themes and movements that are magnificent. And we can do this at any age. A few people can take these inner compositions and turn them into structured and repeatable art forms, such as a Mozart minuet. The closer the music or dance comes to our internal promptings, the greater our enthusiasm. When there is a match between our inner beats and a well-crafted piece of music, we have a march or a waltz, such as the "Beautiful Blue Danube," that seem to comand us to move to their rhythm. But why? I feel this is because they are basically brilliant translations of rhythms we already contain in ourselves.

Modern dance will release your internal rhythms. The problem is that your muscles and skeleton may say, "Who, me?" They will, of course, eventually respond, but first you must coax and tease them into movement. This book shows you how to do that. Liz Lerman believes that everyone can dance. She further believes that each person's movements are beautiful and can be used in meaningful ways to express emotion, re-create an event, deal with an idea, or simply create happiness. In her own work, Liz creates dances filled with energy, humor, and well-articulated moves to comment on personal relationships, religious themes, and political sillinesses.

As a teacher, Liz works with different types of students—from the very young to the very old—to introduce them to modern dance. This book contains her method for turning older people into older dancers. Her method is simple and effective. I speak with double authority. As a specialist in services to older people, I am familiar with the range of programs available in the community. Liz's approach meets all the criteria for appropriateness and acceptability. It is a program that enriches the lives of the participant while holding the individual in the utmost respect. My other source of authority for endorsing this work is my participation, a chunky middle-aged man, in an improvisational dance group that Liz has taught and directed for two years. I know her method works, for I am second to none in awkwardness, yet under her guidance, I dance and I create dances. So do others.

Liz teaches modern dance to a group of older persons in a retirement home. As detailed in this book, she creates a mood of experiment and acceptance among the older dancers in her group. To Liz, there are no bad movements. She can find beauty and excitement in the smallest gesture. Then she helps the dancer expand on the movement. For example, if an older dancer makes a gesture that imitates planting a seed, Liz will appreciate how the dancer moves his hands. Then she will ask the dancer to make the gesture larger, with more movement. Next, she will suggest making the movement smaller and more concise. When the older dancer returns once again to the planting movement, it is more fluid, expressive, and dramatic. In collaboration with the instructor, the older person has created a dance.

What does modern dance mean for the older dancer? It allows the older person to take his or her internal promptings and give them physical expression. It means taking a thought or emotion and working it through in movement. It gives the older person an opportunity to take risks among peers in a safe and protected environment. And, it brings pleasure. These are the benefits of modern dance to the mind and spirit.

There are also benefits to the body that are even more obvious. The stretching and movement that take place in modern dance give full play to the muscles in the body. In this book, Liz gives complete descriptions of exercises that move every part of the body. She starts with exercises that can be done seated, moves on to standing exercises, and graduates to movements in the center of the group. The exercises allow every older person in the group to join in at least some activity. Liz insists that no one be forced to work beyond his or her capacity but that all be encouraged to try. In Liz's class, it is all right to sit out an exercise or a movement.

As older people participate in modern dance, there should be improvements in their range of motion, stamina, and agility. In some cases, participation may stimulate a joy of movement that results in greater physical activity. Whether the result is turning the older person into a disco dancing freak or simply enabling them to tie their shoelaces again, the older person should experience an improvement in bodily movement after some classes in modern dance.

This book is also designed for use by professional dancers who want to extend the dance into the community by working with older people. Part of Liz's philosophy of the dance is that dancers should practice their art among people living in a variety of settings. Liz herself has brought the dance to a senior citizen residence and to a children's hospital. This book is intended to guide the instructor completely through a full program of modern, interpretive dance for the older person.

The book may also be used by nonprofessional dancers. These include persons with some dance training who are now working as recreational or activities directors, physical or occupational therapists, or some other profession in which movement plays a part. The older person with some dance background can also use the book to set up and conduct a modern dance class. The method Liz devised may be used in senior centers, housing for the elderly, or homes for the aged—virtually any place that older persons congregate. The classes can also be held in Ys, community colleges, or neighborhood recreation centers. The prerequisites are a committed teacher, a room large enough to move about in, and a group of interested older persons.

How many potential older dancers are there? It is estimated that over 80 percent of the older population are fully mobile; thus in my opinion, they are physically able to dance. That means there are at least 16 million potential dancers and possibly more. The number of older persons who dance is unknown. My uncle taught dance in 1915, and he still dances three times a week. Any polka party or square dance has its share of older dancers. I estimate that at least 2 million persons over age sixty-five dance for recreation. That means there are still 14 million potential recruits. Admittedly, only a minority of these would be willing to try modern or interpretive dance. Thus, the potential market for modern dance is a "mere" 1.4 million older adults who have yet to try dancing.

How many dance teachers are needed? If each class contained 20 dancers, there could be 70,000 classes meeting each week. If one instructor handled five groups each, there would be 15,000 teachers employed. There are now only a handful, including Liz and her colleagues. While modern dance for older people may never replace ballroom dancing, it can attract a fair sized following.

Imagine older dancers interpreting their experiences and emotions into meaningful movement. Imagine older dancers giving performances in which they confound the stereotypes by creative expression of their knowledge and feelings in a dance form. After reading and using this book, many thousands will perform as older dancers to the enlightenment of themselves and for the enjoyment of many others.

SOLOMON JACOBSON, PH. D.

PREFACE

I AM a dancer. I teach, choreograph, and perform. These facts affect the way I experience the episodes in my life. Seven years ago, my mother died of cancer. While she was sick, we spent hours together talking of our lives. During these conversations, my mind raced with provocative stage images of dancers moving in and out of her landscape. I always imagined older bodies as part of the scene, usually representing long-lost relatives, or I saw pictures of my mother's own body floating Chagall-like through the living room.

After her death, I returned to my home in Washington, D.C., and began to look for older people to fill the needs of this developing dance, and that is what led me to teach dance classes at The Roosevelt for Senior Citizens. I already had experience in working with unconventional dancers, that is to say, people not highly trained but very willing to move, learn, and express with their bodies. By this time in my life, I knew how to find such performers. I would go to a group that already existed for some other purpose and teach modern dance classes, and when a safe emotional environment had been established, I would ask for volunteers to be in a dance.

That is what I did, and after six months of classes, the dance *Woman of the Clear Vision* was premiered. Making that dance reminded me that performance is a wonderful process for building community among people who would not otherwise find themselves together. In this case, while confronting issues about life and death, young people and old people were also able to rehearse and grow as artists, to learn to be comfortable in each other's environment, and to pay attention to each other's lives.

This work with older adults has convinced me of things about dance that I suspected all along — things I knew as a child dancing and things I came to know later as a questioning professional dancer. Dancing, with its expressive and creative aspects, is a natural activity for all human beings. Although the beautifully developed ability of the professional dancer makes for a spectacular display of human potential, it is also true that the inherent characteristics and benefits of dance belong to everyone.

Dance magically combines exercise, self-expression, fun group activity, intellectual stimulation, and spiritual uplift. All people should have access to these activities no matter what their age, ability, or body type.

This work clearly has value for the participants, but it is also important as a symbol of the values a society incorporates for its culture. If art reflects life, certainly it is no surprise to see contemporary dancers pushing for technical virtuosity, for if there is a symbol for our age it must be technology. Dancing artists are no different from anyone else in their urge to achieve efficiency and perfection.

Unfortunately, this places enormous pressure on the development of the technical aspect of dance. There are, however, many other facets of dance to discover, maintain, and develop. They include expressiveness, the exploration of contemporary themes, and the affirmation of a community's deeply felt ties. Older dancers can contribute in these areas.

Senior adults, particularly those who begin studying dance after age sixty, will probably not become fine technical dancers. What they bring to the activity, however, whether it is class warm-ups, improvisation, or informal performing, is an expressive body filled with life experiences. They remind us not only that dance belongs to everyone but that it can speak on many different levels. To ask a senior adult to do a fast, repeatable combination of ballet steps, for example, will mock both the person and the movement itself. But, when that person moves in harmony with an idea or emotion, with a movement vocabulary that is inherently personal in the body, the result is sometimes staggeringly beautiful.

People feel better when they dance. People learn about themselves and their world when they dance. People recognize their limits, strive to overcome them, and can see the results when they dance. These things occur as a person trains to dance. The goal is to develop a person at home in his or her body, a person capable of expressing feelings and ideas through movement, unafraid to move freely in a room filled with people, capable of learning a sequence or structure, willing to try new things, and willing to engage in the simple act of moving for no reason beyond the joy of the experience.

As I have travelled and worked this last decade, I have taught over 3000 dance classes. Everywhere I go I see vast numbers of dancers being trained for a world where no one will pay them to do what they so love to do. The demands of the field wear heavily on many people, clearly emphasizing a narrow definition of dance as a performance art. In the end, for many, the pressures are too great, and they choose to leave dance. With that decision they lose a major part of their lives simply because they did not fit into a precise and rigid structure.

It is hoped that the theory behind the teaching in this book can help younger dancers see that there are alternatives, not just in terms of social rewards and fulfillment as one experiences the joy that dancing can bring to older people but also in the effects this work can have on the dancer herself, as a dancer. There are people to be taught, people who will want to see their dances, people who will want to dance with them. This is in no way compromising to their art, their technique, or their own performing aspirations. It is broadening for everyone.

The significance of this work lies ultimately in its ability to bridge the isolation of artists and of the elderly. The validation and meaning come from positive use of mind and body, the sharing of knowledge, and the resultant joy of people dancing together.

INTRODUCTION

THE PROGRAM

THIS book is based on a program of dance, exercise, and improvisation developed over an eight-year period under the auspices of the Dance Exchange, a nonprofit arts organization I founded in 1976. The Dance Exchange is "an association of dancers who believe that the skills, discipline, expression, and beauty of dance belong to everyone. It is committed to programs and policies that nurture the growth of the individual, the artist, and the community."

The Dance Exchange houses a school and a professional modern dance company called The Dance Exchange Performance Company. It is also a center for an outreach program that extends to hospitals, schools, office buildings, and senior centers.

The project at the Roosevelt developed into a comprehensive program for senior adults that has four components. The first is ongoing modern dance classes open to all residents and guests at various senior centers. The second is the Dancers of the Third Age, an intergenerational touring group open to any older adult who can handle the rigors of the schedule and who wants to perform in this improvisational company. On my invitation, certain older people are invited to join the Dance Exchange Performance Company in formal dance concerts, which is the third part of the work. The fourth component is teacher training, and this takes place through the Dance Exchange in the form of workshops or on an individual basis. Interested organizations who wish to learn more fully about this work have also sponsored one-day workshops or weeklong residencies.

Although the professional or preprofessional dancer has much to gain from participating in a dance program for the elderly, this book is also intended for use by the interested amateur. To many readers who have done only party dancing, dance may seem to be a mystery. Yet, many of the people who would most benefit from use of the information in this book are not dancers. Recreation therapists, activity directors, and administrators of facilities for the elderly may feel that a program such as this would be very helpful to their clients. For those people, the main ingredient to understanding the information in this book is to try all of the movement ideas on their own bodies. They should spend time alone with the exercises and some of the improvisations and see how it feels. They should monitor their own responses to the movement and ask the following questions: Does it feel good? Does it feel silly? Does it seem possible? Does it feel awkward or graceful? Is it fun?

In answering these questions, instructors will be able to project in part how their dance students will feel. It is also true that the more a movement makes sense to one's own body, the more it will work with others. If instructors already have exercise classes going, they should simply incorporate a little of the new information in each class and go only as far as it seems right to them.

In addition to dancers, recreation therapists, activity directors, nurses, and administrators, this book can be used by individuals who are looking for a form of exercise, relaxation, and enjoyable use of their bodies. Although it is easier to stay active by dancing in a group, it is also possible to do much of this alone.

Older people who may have danced in their younger days may find these ideas stimulating. They make very fine dance class leaders because they can draw on their own experience as well as learn new skills and techniques.

Chapter One deals with the question, Why modern dance for senior adults? A brief definition of the different kinds of dance will be offered so that the reader can understand how modern dance can borrow from the other forms but in the end can have its own reason for success.

Chapter Two addresses the theory of these classes. The discussion includes attitudes of positive support that must permeate the environment of a dance class. Particular emphasis is placed on requiring the dancer to adapt traditional dance movement to the needs of the students without feeling personally compromised, or condescending.

The administrative setup is the focus of Chapter Three. Attention is given to the relationship between teachers and other people at the senior center, funding support, and the little extras such as live musical accompaniment, which can make such a difference in the success of these classes.

The next four chapters explain and describe a typical modern dance class for senior adults. They take the student from warm-up on the chair, to standing exercises, and finally to work with improvisation and performance.

Chapter Eight describes performing as a development of class work. This leads into Chapter Nine, which assesses the benefits of the program for young and old. Included are remarks by participants reflecting on what has happened to them as they have come to dance.

Chapter Ten is a summary and describes research needs for the future.

Dancing for older people works. The program will grow as fast as the teacher takes it. Whether that teacher is a dancer, activity director, movement therapist, or very interested amateur, it is hoped that this book will help bring dance and its vitality to many senior adults. They in turn will have another environment and medium through which to share the richness of their lives.

ACKNOWLEDGMENTS

MANY people have participated in making this book a reality. It is impossible to mention every dancer, administrator, volunteer, audience person, and friend by name, but I can say thank you to all of you.

My family has supported the ideas, struggle, and development of each stage of my work. So, to Sarah Dean, David and Sharon Lerman, Richard, Joshua, and Jesse Lerman, and the Spelman family, I say thanks. My sisters-in-law, Saf Lerman and Victoria Spelman have given me extra encouragement as a woman writing. My father, Philip E. Lerman deserves special thanks for insisting that I be a dancer who thinks. My husband, Jon Spelman has spent many hours listening, comforting, advising, challenging, and even proof reading, and to him I simply say thank you.

The Dance Exchange community, its dancers, staff, students, board of directors, volunteers, and friends have all contributed extraordinary amounts of energy, commitment, and hard work to making the theory of this book come alive. Among those people are Marty Belin, Diane Bernstein, Nancy Cole, Dennis DeLoria, Carol Dunn, Liesel Flashenberg, Bob Fogelgren, Diane Hull Ganshauer, Elliot Maxwell, Joan Millen, Ron McClain, Daniel Nachtigal, Jim Patterson, Helen Rea, Sophie Reuther, Jill Shellow, Kate Stephansky, Rima Wolff, and Don Zuckerman. Jeff Bliss, Mary Buckley, Debra Caplowe, Diane Floyd, Keith Goodman, and Ann MacDonald also contributed many hours of rehearsal so that intergenerational dances could happen. My thanks to these people and everyone who has touched this program.

Organizations and people in the Washington, D.C., area who have nurtured this program and helped in its development deserve special recognition. They are Alix Cohn, Patrick Hayes, Bea Prosterman, and Douglas Wheeler of the Washington Performing Arts Society; Susan Eidenberg, director of New Horizons at Children's Hospital, National Medical Center; Janice McKelvey of the Community Service Program and Mary Francis Pearson, Chairman of the Education Committee, both of the Wolf Trap Foundation; Martha Ramsey of the American Association of Retired Persons; Jackie Sunderland of the National Council on the Aging; and the administrative staff of The Roosevelt for Senior Citizens. James Breen of George Washington University supported the earliest visions of this work and continues to provide a place for exploration.

Special thanks to Doctor Nancy Johnson, whose skills as an academic advisor made writing about this subject both a challenge and a joy. The District of Columbia Commission on the Arts and Humanities' Special Constituencies Program and the Expansion Arts Program of the National Endowment for the Arts are two agencies which have provided funding for part of this work. I am respectful and thankful to all of these institutions.

Special friends and teachers whose ideas and work contributed directly to this book include Don Adams, Arlene Goldbard, Deborah Lamb, Sally Nash, Delfa Vaznaugh, and Arthur Waskow and Florence West.

Arnold Kramer has generously made available all the photographs of the work sessions that so beautifully accompany the text. All photographs not specifically noted are his. Thelma Tulane and Ada Welch graciously performed as models for his work. Jess Rea and Judith Jourdin also gave extra time for photographic sessions. Dr. Solomon Jacobson provided editorial assistance and encouragement at just the right time. I also want to thank Florence West, a very great dance teacher who helped me to understand the discipline and freedom of my art.

Finally, I want to thank the group of people without whom none of this would have been possible, the older people of Washington, D.C., who allowed themselves to be my students and my teachers. I especially want to recognize those who worked in productions and performance. Thank you Harry Belanger, Rebecca Finkelstein, Vee Hallenbeck, Betty Harris, Louise Haskins, John Johnson, Judith Jourdin, Lee Legal, Lenore Mayo, Mary Mylecraine, Olena Olhofsky, Elizabeth Pendleton, Edward Powell, Jess Rea, Betty Rothenberg, Charles Rother, Thelma Tulane, Ada Welch, and Anna Mary Wells.

CONTENTS

Page

Foreword by Anna Halprin vii

Foreword by Solomon Jacobson ix

Preface xiii

Introduction xvii

Chapter

One WHY MODERN DANCE FOR SENIOR ADULTS?   3

Two BASIC THEORY AND DEFINITION OF TERMS   6

Three HOW, WHERE, WHEN, AND WHO IS GOING TO PAY FOR IT?   10

Four THE BEGINNING OF CLASS: WARM—UP   20

Five STANDING WARM—UPS   74

Six MOVING INTO THE CENTER: IMPROVISATION   94

Seven MORE CENTER WORK 116

Eight PUBLIC DEMONSTRATION AND PERFORMANCE:

THE DANCERS OF THE THIRD AGE 123

Nine BENEFITS FOR OLDER AND YOUNGER DANCERS 139

Ten REFLECTIONS ON THE FUTURE 149

Bibliography 157

Index 159

TEACHING DANCE
TO
SENIOR ADULTS

Chapter One

WHY MODERN DANCE
FOR SENIOR ADULTS?

W E know that exercise is good for people. All of the joggers, dancercisers, and TV fitness fanatics and the millions of Americans who participate in some kind of regular recreation can attest to the well-being that comes from physical activity. The elderly, too, need programs designed to meet their special needs and still allow them to gain the better mental and physical health derived from regular exercise. Research indicates that there is a need for such programs. Dance is a wonderful form of physical activity that goes beyond exercise to involve the emotional, spiritual, and social self, but what kind of dance works, and why particularly modern dance?

There are many ways to dance, and many kinds of dancing. Moving alone in one's room responding to music or to an intense personal experience is a kind of dance. So is the highly stylized technical brilliance of a ballet company. The spectrum includes disco, interpretive dance, improvisation, ethnic dances, and many more, including TV commercials that feature dancing. What they have in common, to a greater or lesser degree, are the concepts and images we as people project onto body movement in order to call it dance.

In describing and defining movement as dance, people use words such as *joy, expression, graceful, moving to music, sweaty, routine, stretch, groups of people moving together, relaxation*. However one describes dance, it is clear that a dance-related activity can be a part of the life experience of people of all ages.

Despite the commonality of dance forms, there are differences among the various styles and types of dance. The distinctions will affect the actual experience of the activity, the context in which it happens, and the product. These differences originate in the motivation of the dancer, needs of the group, and the goals of the activity.

In her book *Dance from Magic to Art*, Lois Ellfeldt (1976) defines the multitude of dance forms that have evolved to meet contemporary society. She defines modern dance in three categories: interpretive, classical, and contemporary. The interpretive, or creative, form she defines as a natural movement style that represents a new freedom (pp. 116-117). The classical modern dance is defined in terms of the choreographers who sought to find material that reflected a social consciousness and internal feelings (p. 122). She sees the contemporary modern dance as still forming. Its characteristics include using movement for its own sake so that it has a logic without having to tell a story or be emotional (p. 123).

The program described in this book is a synthesis of the interpretive, classical, and contemporary modes of modern dance. It provides a wide spectrum of activities from which student and teacher can choose depending on their needs, expectations, and abilities. Older people can be challenged by the discipline and tradition of a dance form, as well as by a confrontation with the freedom that exploring new movement possibilities can bring.

In modern dance, one is faced with technical demands as in other dance forms, but a person can also develop new movement vocabularies based on the needs and motivation of the choreographer or on the student's own interests and abilities. Modern dance is not steeped in a rigid tradition; it relates to fundamental ideas found in other systems of dance.

There are also many ways to experience dance. In our culture we are accustomed to viewing dance as audience members. The young sometimes take dance classes, but generally only the dedicated continue dance training. Few people have an ongoing participation with dance. This is unfortunate for several reasons. Participation at the amateur level increases appreciation for dance performance. More importantly, experiencing a modern dance class leads a person to discover many things. The technical training teaches physical control and provides a framework to explore a wide range of movement possibilities. Confronting one's physical limitations and learning how to extend beyond them create a new knowlege and appreciation of the body.

The improvisational element of a modern dance class can teach freedom of expression and an ability to relate to other people in a physical way. Here the relationship between the imagination and the physical representation of that imagination develops a partnership between mind and body that is very exciting.

Through performance, whether it is an informal classroom exercise or a more formal learned repertory piece, one can acquire a sense of confidence and achievement. The approval from the audience brings a sense of well-being. The viewer's attention creates an intensity that sometimes provokes a deeper understanding of the material and the self.

Experiencing all these elements of modern dance offers a person a physical, thoughtful, and giving way to be in a group. At any one moment, however, a person may wish to become private, and the focus of the work can become internal. This is the true gift of dance. It is simultaneously a solo or group activity, a private or public encounter.

THERAPY AND ART

Throughout history, dance has been used as a way to communicate feelings and ideas. In the early twentieth century, through the efforts of modern dance pioneer Isadora Duncan, there was a renaissance in dance. In a direct revolt against the highly stylized balletic movement of the period, Duncan made people aware of the innate, natural qualities of dance. She spoke of its relationship to the "soul," or inner being.

As modern dance developed, some people began to look more closely at the relationship between movement and emotions. Since dance could be about feeling, it seemed logical to assume that it might be used as a tool to help therapists unlock the feelings of their clients. This investigation gained momentum and professional interest, and by the end of the World War II, the field of dance therapy had become a valid therapeutic tool.

Dance therapy employs dance to aid the mental growth of the client, who is often institutionalized or in some way very isolated from society. Some dance therapists work with senior adults. There are ways in which modern dance classes for the elderly are similar to the program that a dance therapist might run. For example, both are done in groups, feelings are explored, and the actual movement produced might appear the same. The two approaches are, however, different in goals, expectations, and agreement between teacher and student.

Modern dance classes focus on the experience of dance rather than the therapeutic growth of the individual. A dance teacher will be concerned with the growth of the participants, but it is not the sole guiding factor in the class development. Likewise, a dance therapist is probably less interested in an aesthetic or artistic product or process. Interestingly enough, the dance process is therapeutic, but the product is not therapy.

Art can also concern itself with the development of the human being. It, too, can function to help integrate the individual and allow for the growth of the artist and the society around him or her. In fact, most artists would agree that a major reason they continue to work in their field is for personal satisfaction, self-understanding, and intellectual growth. However, art goes beyond self-interest, and as John Dewey said, "It gestures towards a public reality."

Chapter Two

BASIC THEORY AND DEFINITION
OF TERMS

L EARNING to dance provides many benefits for the older person, and the
senior citizen center can be a very special training ground for the younger,
as well as the older, dancer. Many relationships can unfold in this setting.
Teacher to student, dancer to new audience, young to life experienced are some
of the ways that both generations can build a mutual support system, bringing
a fresh outlook to everyone.

Several basic principles are involved in bringing modern dance to a senior
center. Following these principles will ensure that relationships will thrive.

First, everyone can dance. The teacher must absolutely accept this fact in order
to contradict the feelings that some older adults may carry. Not only are older
people saddled with the usual set of negative body images — "I'm too fat; I
have two left feet; I'm clumsy; I can't keep a beat" — but they have additional
stereotypes to battle — "Old people should be careful and sit still." "How can
they remember anything? They're senile, crippled, and forgetful and have the
attention span of a child." These all contribute to the notions of the old as non-
movers.

*Second, if the classes are to succeed, a teacher must respond to the beauty and capability
of each student.* This acceptance is not difficult to do, since the dances of these
students are, in fact, beautiful. If teachers have stereotyped ideas of what
graceful, pretty, or expressive movement is, then they will have to change. Any
preconceived notion of perfect form will get in the way of seeing the senior
adult dancers for what they are capable of doing.

Some people might find the absolute validation of each student's movement
as misleading or dishonest. Supporting people's ability in a positive way does
not mean there is no room for correction. It does not mean compromising one's
goals. It does mean that the instructor must meet the student where he or she
is, comment on what is already available to the student, and develop in the student the awareness of potentially doing more.

There will be times when the teacher is frustrated. Respecting older students does not mean hiding from them the very real feelings that any teacher has. It is appropriate to find a way to let the students know of anger or disappointments while maintaining the absolute expectation that they will succeed.

Third, each person should dance as well as he or she can. This applies to both teacher and student. Some dancers feel that their performing well will depress their students, but one should not disguise one's natural ability because students are novices. The difficulty of this situation is compounded for some younger teachers because they know their older students may never reach a high level of technical virtuosity. It is important, however, that the teacher dance his or her best no matter what the movement activity is. It is condescending to do less. The younger dancer can find many ways to dance beautifully without discouraging the students. In fact, this is one of the challenges of this work.

Fourth, it is necessary for the teacher to adapt traditional dance movement to the technical capabilities of the student. This must be done in a way that is honest for the teacher and challenging for the student. The teacher needs to ask what is important for the older dancer to accomplish. Sometimes the answer is the same for any dance student; sometimes it is not. This decision affects what the teacher chooses to emphasize in class. For instance, it may be important in a second position plié to insist that the knees go over the feet, since that is a way to insure safety, but it might not be important to stress the classically straight spine while a student does the warm-up, since this may be an issue of taste or style.

Fifth, the work must be mutually beneficial to both instructor and dancer. The senior center setting forces a dancer to decide what is important about dance and how to communicate that to people who may have very stereotyped views of what dance actually is. This program will not succeed, however, if one pursues it strictly as "something good for them, for the older person." The dancer must be open to the learning experience that awaits him or her. The art of dance can flourish where people are excited to try it, full of questions about how to do it, and feeling good enough and confident enough to dance in front of others.

These five ideas — believing that everyone can dance, accepting the efforts of students, prompting everyone to do the best he or she can, adapting movement without compromise to the form, and ensuring that there is something in it for both dancer and participant — are crucial to this program.

In addition to these basic concepts there are several terms in need of clear definition.

BASIC TERMS

Art is an activity that combines technical training, expressiveness, and a sense of aesthetics to present a point of view. The activity usually involves dance, theatre, painting, sculpture, video, literature, or multimedia and is presented by the artist to the rest of society.

A *modern dance class* is a class of movement that begins with a warm-up, progresses to a series of steps put together in a repeatable form, and then includes improvisational structures in which participants can seek their own movement responses to particular stimuli in order to fulfill tasks, communicate an idea, or simply move. The actual movement vocabulary may originate in ballet or several techniques developed in this country through the pioneering work of Martha Graham, Merce Cunningham, and José Limón. The teaching may also derive its source material from theater, mime, and the constantly inventive movement ideas developing in modern dance.

Improvisation is a way of designing movement experiences so that they happen on the spot, that is, a dancer or dancers make the dance up at the moment. There are many ways to develop improvisation, and these varied approaches are often called structures, or scripts. An improvisational script can be very open, such as, "Dance however you want until you are tired." A structure can also be closed, or at least more defined, such as, "Move for sixty seconds on a diagonal path changing levels twice."

There are several reasons to improvise. The basic assumption of improvisation is that one's own unique movement style or vocabulary is valid. Thus, improvising finds ways to explore each person's unique movement vocabulary. Improvisation can also highlight a dancer's movement patterns and tendencies. If one can determine characteristic habits, one can also develop improvisational structures that help a person expand into new areas of movement.

Choreographers use improvisation to find movement ideas or to develop them. Dancers use improvisation to have fun, to work out or loosen up, and to maintain access to spontaneity.

For people new to dance, or for people who have been highly trained in the classical tradition, improvisation can seem very difficult. Often, in the beginning, these people find themselves thinking only of their inhibition and their repetitive patterns or that the dances they are making are ugly or dumb.

With a supportive and skilled teacher and a safe emotional environment to work in, it is relatively easy to overcome these feelings and find that dancing improvisationally is a natural response to life issues and that moving alone or in a group within a structure can be a fulfilling experience.

Performances may be of several kinds. All have the following in common: there is a performer and at least one observer. The performer knows that a specific activity is happening and that he or she is being watched. The audience members know that they are giving their attention to an activity as observers.

An *informal performance* is one in which most of the dances are openly structured, allowing for improvisation and mistakes. Natural lighting and everyday clothes are used. The audience is often a group that has been organized for some other purpose, such as students at a school, people attending a conference, or senior adults gathered at a nutrition site.

A *formal concert* is a dance with a set structure, costumes, and formal lighting and often with special designers. It requires many hours of rehearsal and a technical schedule for staging. The press is invited to review it, and an admission fee is charged.

With these broad definitions in mind, it is possible to proceed to the practical issues facing dancers, administrators, and participants of a modern dance program in a senior center.

Chapter Three

HOW, WHERE, WHEN, AND WHO IS GOING TO PAY FOR IT?

COMMITMENT, skills, and a desire to teach are the basis of a dance program for senior adults, but even the best of intentions must be housed in a structure that supports the work. A dancer or consultant who comes to work at a senior center part time must understand the context in which the class is taking place. The full-time activity director needs to recognize the special requirements of a dance class in order to establish an ongoing program. Understanding these issues will contribute to the success of a dance class for senior adults.

TYPES OF SENIOR CENTERS

There are several types of senior centers. Each varies according to the services provided, the hours of operation, and the health and activity level of the participants. Although generalizations can be made about the kinds of senior centers and the way to program dance for each one, ultimately it will be up to the staff or consultant at each center to adapt the ideas to meet the needs of each place. Dance can play a special role in each type of center.

Residences

A long-term care facility can be part of a hospital or nursing home and is a place where the older people usually have some sort of chronic ailment or impairment. In these settings the dance classes must use music as a way of allowing involvement for many of the people who will only participate in small ways. Most of the dancing will take place in chairs. The teacher will need to do a lot of one-on-one work with each person in the class. Frequent touching will also help to keep individuals alert and involved in the class. Although many find the initial idea of dancing in this type of facility peculiar or strange, it can be very uplifting for residents and staff alike.

Independent apartments with communal dining, such as the Roosevelt for Senior Citizens, is a second category of residence, which offers active adults who need some support in their daily lives a place to maintain an independent life-style. These facilities vary with the kinds of services they provide. Nearly all include meals. Usually laundry, grocery stores, some health or drug stores, and beauty shops are franchised within the buildings. Some places, such as the Roosevelt, do not have nursing staffs, and individuals may hire private help. This means that the activity level of the residents varies widely, from those who are still working every day to those who are trying desperately to avoid a nursing home.

Because so many of the ideas in this book were developed at the Roosevelt, it seems useful to add a bit more information about it. The Roosevelt for Senior Citizens provides independent apartment living and communal dining for the elderly. It is located in downtown Washington, D.C. Between 300 and 400 people live there at one time, with income levels from low to upper middle. Many of the people at the Roosevelt are ambulatory, and although they have chosen this in-town living situation for its convenience, they rarely go out. The contrasts among the elderly at the Roosevelt are great. Some hold a job, drive a car, or make regular use of the nearby bus system. Others always stay inside, not even venturing outdoors for the field trips that the management operates for a fee about once a month.

Retirement villages are adult residential communities open to people of retirement age or older. There are usually many activity programs available.

Nonresidential Sites

Activity centers are multipurpose senior centers offering educational and social programs. They link the older person to services in the community.

Nutrition sites are often organized by churches or synagogues. These centers include activities around the noon meal. Frequently the hours of operation are from 10 AM to 2 PM. They are social in nature, and only some provide additional programming beyond the meal itself.

Social centers are often sponsored by church groups. Depending on the staffing, mission of the organization, and commitment of the sponsoring group, these centers can run half or full days, several times a week or daily. The programs vary tremendously, but learning activities and field trips are usually a main staple.

Day care facilities provide programs aimed at the severely impaired older adult who still lives at home with family. These facilities take the older person for the day. Many activities are appropriate in these settings, including dance classes.

Day hospital programs are similar to day care, except that they may be run for shorter amounts of time. These might center around a particular disease or problem such as Alzheimer's groups. Depending on the program, appropriate therapeutic and recreational and artistic programs can be established.

ARRANGEMENTS IN THE SENIOR CENTERS

Scheduling Time

Dance classes can be useful at any location. At a residence such as the Roosevelt, they become part of the social calendar and take place in the evening after dinner. By 7 PM some people are too tired to attend, but most like the combination of entertainment and exercise and consider the class a help in preparing them for sleep.

For people who gather at nutrition sites, the dance class may be the only activity other than the noontime meal. It is best to dance before eating. The only problem with this is that people's interest in lunch will erode the last fifteen minutes of class. Usually it is good to end these classes early to avoid distraction.

At centers dedicated to providing all-day activities for older people, the dance class can take place at any time. Here the only problem is competition. Very often in this site, there are so many activities to choose from that it is difficult to maintain the same class participants from week to week. Whatever the situation is, care must be taken to schedule the class at a time when people are free to try it.

Where to Hold Class

Finding the best place in the center for the dance class is important. Several factors affect that decision. Size of the group, need for privacy, noise, and the location of musical resources will help determine the best location for dancing.

Often, the largest clear, open space in a center or residence is a common room that is used for many purposes. This is advantageous since people are used to congregating there. There is plenty of room for dancers and onlookers. Usually these rooms are centrally located so that passersby, staff, and visitors can watch comfortably. It is best to have the backs of the participants face towards the corridor or entryway to a room. This way they can concentrate on the dancing without being aware of who is watching, coming, and going. The teacher will also be in a position to monitor the activity level in the hall or doorway and can quiet it down if it gets too noisy.

Using public space for a dance class will have an effect on nonparticipants in the center, including staff. It might take time for everyone to accept the class and recognize its value. For example, originally at the Roosevelt, kitchen help, engineers, and some of the administration thought it was funny to see the older people dancing. They have come to understand its benefits and even join the class now and then. Because of this understanding it is easier to get cooperation for scheduling, which is necessary in a center where so much is happening.

Distracting Noise in the Center

A dance teacher in a senior center must assume from the beginning that this class will not be quiet as in conventional schools. Noise comes from everywhere. It can be a problem for participants in the dance class and for people engaged in other activities in the center. This can be a delicate issue, and care should be taken early in the sessions to solve any disagreements about use of the space. The dance class can also be noisy. Although most nonparticipants will enjoy the music, they might find the loud encouragement of the teacher or the spontaneous sounds of the dancers to be distressing. The dancers, on the other hand, can be distracted by bingo games or loud laughter from nearby card playing.

This is not a hopeless situation, however. Like most issues facing a teacher in this environment, choices can be made based on goals, balancing the needs of the students and the requirements of dance training. In time, students and teacher alike learn to concentrate in this very active environment.

The conversations, mutterings, and ongoing commentary by class members may be a new experience for the teacher and takes getting used to. If one listens, it can be very helpful. Often the comments made quietly to a neighbor or to no one in particular can let the teacher know what the students are experiencing. When the behavior is disturbing and has nothing to do with the class, it is important for the teacher to stop it. This can be done by asking people to wait until class is over to carry on their conversation, or the teacher may sense that the students need a rest and lead a short group discussion for a while instead of dancing. Sometimes it is possible to turn the disruption into a dance phrase. For example, once two women erupted into a loud argument. The class stopped and did some punching movements from the warm-up series. Then they improvised angry dances. After five minutes, the class was back on track, and the two women were participating again.

It is necessary to balance the merits of having observers in the classroom with the noise that invariably comes from people who are not fully participating. In the long run, it is very useful for them, and the center as a whole, to encourage people to come to watch the class. For some, it is the only way they can involve themselves. For example, there is a regular onlooker at the Roosevelt. She comes each week and watches class, occasionally talking quietly with anyone near her. After class she always thanks the teacher and says, "I did it all in my imagination."

How Private Should the Dance Class Be?

The need for privacy depends on the kind of work one wants to accomplish. In a large room with many people participating at different levels of involvement, the class will be more social in nature. If a major goal is to involve as many people as possible, it makes sense to hold a public class.

If, however, the teacher wants to work on more intense themes or challenge the group to explore areas that might cause them embarrassment, it is probably useful to find a more secluded location in the center. At the Roosevelt, small group rehearsals are often held in the TV room on the eighth floor. In this private space people feel safe enough to improvise on themes such as sexuality, anger, and getting older. They also feel OK about making mistakes, trying new material, and talking with each other about the work, but the main class takes place in a larger public room on the first floor.

Size of the Group

The size of the group will affect the dance experience. Large groups are exciting since they are energetic. Often, just seeing lots of people dancing will entice others to try it. A small group can allow for corrections, response to people's questions, and a deeper awareness of individual progress. The decision to limit class size can be the teacher's or the administrator's, but the class will have to adapt depending on the number of people involved. Once a group is larger than ten, much of the leader's attention will shift from individual needs to group dynamics.

Musical Accompaniment

Music is wonderful to have in a modern dance class but is not essential. What kind of music and when to use it depend on the teacher's goals. If simply getting people up and moving is the primary goal, then selecting popular music or familiar melodies will certainly bring pleasure and ease of involvement to the group. A caution, however, is that music will impose the style of dance. If one plays a waltz, people will grab partners and waltz. Disco will send a few to their feet mimicking TV dance, while folk dances or a march will produce their own obvious outcomes.

Teaching without music is also an option. It requires that a teacher be comfortable with this mode and be able to explain to the students the benefits of dancing without musical support. Some students find it liberating to realize that they have their own internal rhythms and that things other than music can motivate movement. Usually a mixture of silence and music proves to be an effective stimulus.

The best solution to the music problem is to have an accompanist. Musicians who play flute, guitar, drums, or piano have all been successful in classes for senior adults. The musician should be skilled in improvisational accompaniment, although these classes can be a good training ground for someone who is sensitive and quick with his or her instrument. In this situation, an accompanist can provide the changing rhythm of the warm-ups and support the unique improvisational dances that students devise later in class. In addition, if a particular movement experience can benefit from familiar music, then that, too, can be provided by the skilled musician.

The choice of music may affect the location of the class. Obviously if a pianist is used, then the class should be held near the piano. If a record player is the choice of accompaniment, then the class must be where the equipment is easily accessible.

Seating Arrangements

Since the first part of the class is done while sitting, it is necessary to have plenty of room between each chair so that the arms can be held out from the sides of the body. The problem with this is that people feel far apart from each other. Occasionally people may want to hold hands as part of a chair dance, and the distance precludes this. Once again, the teacher must decide, with the feedback from students, what makes the most sense. At the Roosevelt, people have chosen to keep the chairs closer together and to stretch their arms in directions that will not hit anyone.

In large classes of thirty to fifty, the chairs are arranged in several rows of semicircles to accommodate everyone. In smaller classes, one circle of chairs is usually adequate. This way, everyone can see the teacher and each other. This is important since there are several times during class when it is necessary to follow people other than the teacher.

Sitting in a circle allows everyone to feel part of the group, but it does raise an interesting issue for a dance teacher, the question of left and right. If the teacher identifies movement by saying "left arm," it is practically impossible to have all participants get it correctly if they are sitting in a circle. The problem is compounded if the teacher demonstrates the movement; people facing the teacher will mirror her or him. If she or he lifts the left arm, the logical one for them to lift is the right. No amount of discussion seems to remedy the situation. What is worse is that often participants end up feeling stupid because they cannot get something as basic as left and right.

This situation can be resolved by designing dance movement in such a way that it does not matter which arm goes up. If at some point it is important, then do not sit in a circle that day. Put the chairs in rows facing the same direction. Then, when demonstrating, everyone will be able to mirror correctly without confusion.

In some senior adult groups it is therapeutically important for the participants to be able to recognize right and left and achieve success in this. A prop such as a scarf can be used to help. If everyone ties a scarf on the left arm then the teacher can call for the scarf to be moved.

Publicity to Gain Interest in the Class

There are several ways to attract people to the first class. Giving a name to the activity is important and should be discussed with the administrator of the center. Although the class is modern dance, sometimes including the word *exercise* in the title will make it more attractive. Once people are committed to the class, explanations of the differences between dance and exercises are helpful. The Roosevelt lists the class as "dance exercises."

If the center has a newsletter, then it is important to publish an article or announcement about the class. Brightly colored flyers can also help bring people to the first class. These can be posted near elevators, in the dining room, and even slipped under the door of each person's room if the management approves.

The Dance Exchange starts a series of classes in a new location with a performance by the Dancers of the Third Age. This demonstrates the joy and excitement of dancing and inspires the older people to see what others of their generation are doing. If such a group is not available, the teacher should consider the possibility of arranging a performance by a local modern dance group. If they warm up in front of the audience and explain a little of what they are performing, it might also create some interest among the elderly.

Clothing for Participants and Teachers

People will arrive at class wearing clothing that is comfortable to them but not necessarily comfortable for dancing. Most have probably not participated in any kind of dance class before and might not have considered that pants are better than skirts and full dresses are better than straight ones. Likewise, a barefoot teacher wearing leotards and tights might cause amusement, indignation, or shock.

Unless the teacher has very strong feelings about certain attire, it is fine to allow each person to dress in his or her own way. Often this means adapting the movement to the clothes. For example, any movement requiring the legs to open wide is impossible for most of the women who wear straight dresses. The instructor should continue to do the movement, while suggesting that they do it smaller.

Many older people are conscious of their feet. Their doctors have told them to wear certain shoes. Others maintain a fashionable style even though it might cause pain and discomfort, especially in a dance class. These people can be gently encouraged to wear flat-heeled shoes. However, it is often difficult to get some people to change their shoes. The dance teacher needs to watch these developments. If some students continue to wear higher heels to class, the teacher can change the movements, ask people not to participate, or make sure the student is stable on her feet.

Consistency of Attendance

Very often students are exhilarated after the first few dance classes. It is surprising and disappointing, then, when they do not return to class, but teachers should not get discouraged. There are reasons students discontinue classes, and there are ways to encourage them to return.

Dancing is a new experience for older people. It contradicts many of their expected living patterns, and that can be scary. Suddenly they find themselves becoming active, laughing, enjoying younger people, and feeling good. These feelings may make the rest of the week too hard to bear, so they stop coming to class.

Dancing itself can be a vulnerable experience. During the class it is quite possible to trigger a memory with a particular movement or familiar music. Also, improvisation can touch a subject that the student finds painful to contemplate, much less to dance. This threatens students enough to keep them away.

Not every person in a senior center will participate in dance classes. Those who do not might make fun of those who do, and depending on the personalities involved, the ostracism is enough to keep some from returning to class.

A teacher needs to be resourceful and comfortable about asking people to come back to class. A phone call just reminding them of the time of the class will help. Letting them know that they are missed is sometimes all that is necessary. Even committed dancers will miss class occasionally. After one absence it is not always easy to come back, but it is always useful to welcome people back after they have been absent and give them support during class. The teacher should go over material slowly so that those who have been sporadic in attendance have more of a chance to be a part of the group. After a while, a very solid core group will form as regular students, and they will help with the reminders, the recruitment, and the general enthusiasm for the class.

Administration

The administrator of the center is an important person in this project. It is essential that he or she support the idea that older people can dance and work for the success of the class. Usually this is not a problem, since the positive benefits to the entire center are usually well understood by the staff. This means not scheduling competitive activities or special events during class time. The dance class must be consistent if it is to succeed, and administrators must understand this. It is also helpful if they allow other staff or custodial people the time to enjoy the class, either by watching or participating.

Although it is not necessary for the administrator to dance, to be a dancer, or even to be interested in dance, it is vital for him or her to believe that physical activity is good for the older adult. These classes can be affected negatively by an administrator who is unhappy with his or her own body or feels embarrassed by seeing older people dance.

Frequently the dance teacher, who only comes to the center once or twice a week, becomes a popular figure. Sometimes this charisma is threatening to an administrator who is stuck with the daily problems of running the center. Again, this can cause problems for a class through indifference to the needs of the teacher or students, by overscheduling, or by cancellation.

A relationship that allows for open communication between the teacher and administrator is crucial. Often issues arise that take time to work out. For example, it is likely that some people not involved in the class will find the dancing noisy, silly, or offensive. Being available to meet with the staff and the unhappy residents might make the difference whether a class continues or not. It is therefore part of the teacher's job to expect to spend extra time on the site of the class to ensure a good relationship.

Funding for the Class

Senior citizen centers have been relying on volunteers for years. This is especially true in the areas of arts, social activity, and recreation. Continuing research indicates that new and creative programs for the elderly are necessary. This means hiring professionals to carry out the projects, and that means money.

If a senior center decides to have its own activity director teach the class, then it is important to budget time and money so that he or she can continue dance training. This will keep movement ideas fresh and allow the director time to improve his or her own dancing.

Whether the cost is for a professional dancer or for the activity director's time, money does need to be raised. In a time of economic insecurity such as we face now, this task might seem formidable, but it is not impossible.

Money can be raised by the dancer and his or her arts organization, if he or she has one, or by the sponsoring senior center. Some services that have responded include the following: (1) Government subsidy including grants from the Departments of Health and Human Services and Housing and Urban Development. The grant from the latter was from the housing department in a neighboring county. The classes were held in government-run senior citizen housing projects. (2) Local arts commission grants for special constituencies. (3) Private donations. (4) Fund-raising activity in the center with participants baking, sewing, and so forth to raise the money. (5) The National Endowment for the Arts.

Record Keeping by the Teacher

Two kinds of records are useful in order to document the program, its development, and the creative process involved. The first is numerical. It is important to keep a record of the number of participants. Sponsors, foundations, and other interested people will want to know how many people take the class and how many request its continuation.

The teacher should also keep a notebook concerned with the details, plans, successes, and failures of each class. There are so many small, yet intense, moments in this kind of teaching that the instructor will want a way to refer back to them. Stories older people tell seem so significant that one thinks one will never forget them, but without a comment in a noteboook, even the best story is easily lost.

The students, too, can be encouraged to keep notes or at least have open discussions while the teacher takes notes. This not only ensures feedback for the teacher but documents an important part of the story.

Medical Records

The relationship of dance to physical and emotional well-being is a controversial subject, but dancers are not trained physicians. The older dancers will ask many questions about their bodies and their physical pains. A teacher may be called upon to answer them but should make sure to tell the person to consult a doctor, too.

Before a class series begins, a dancer must have three things: insurance, accident policy, and a clear understandiing with the sponsor about the health of the participants in the class. Insurance may be carried by the teacher or by the sponsoring organization. For example, the Dance Exchange is covered by the insurance of each sponsoring organization, as well as maintaining its own policy. It is probably safest, though, to make sure that the center has adequate coverage in the case of accident. According to some lawyers, a written release statement saying that the students take the class at their own risk is not necessarily effective in court.

Accident policy refers to the way each center wants to handle emergencies. The instructor should find out whether the person in charge should stay with the injured person or leave to make a phone call. The dance teacher should also make sure emergency numbers are quickly available and know who on the administrative staff is to be called. It is important to discuss carefully with the staff what they think is the best way to handle the rest of the group in time of emergency.

Each center will have its own policy regarding pre-dance-class checkups. In some cases, seniors are not allowed to take the class unless their doctors approve. In other centers, there is no consent form needed, and the teacher is free to teach whoever comes. In either case, it is good to discuss with a staff person the health of any individual one feels cautious about. One should ask if any people in the group are under specific instructions from their doctors and for details about each class member so that one feels secure in helping the students make judgments about the best physical activity level for them.

With the preliminaries decided, it is time to begin.

Chapter Four

THE BEGINNING OF
CLASS: WARM-UP

M ANY students arrive at the first class not knowing what to expect. There are things a teacher can do to make them more comfortable. First, the teacher should greet each person warmly and shake hands. These greetings become a kind of ritual, a time when teacher and student can share personal stories or current events. It is important to get to class early enough to ensure time for these encounters.

Some older people are very attached to their pocketbooks, bag, or the loose room keys they carry. Gently ask them to place their belongings under the chair and reassure them that the items will be there when class is over. This might have to be repeated each week.

It is very helpful to have assistants available. These might be other dancers, friends of the teacher who are interested in the work, family members of the students (if they do not mind), and other seniors who are either very interested or very strong. The role of the assistant varies and can be anything from just another presence in the class to active partner in dancing. If the assistants are younger people or folks who otherwise do not belong at the center, they should also introduce themselves to each person every week.

REMINDERS TO TEACHERS

The five general comments that follow are thoughts to keep in mind throughout the class.

1. Moving is good. The absolute underlying concept in these classes is that it is natural, healthy, and satisfying to dance. No other reason is necessary.

2. All people will do what they are able to and then stop. It is important to validate each person's participation no matter how much of the class he or she dances. Only when people feel OK about sitting out for a few minutes will the teacher be able to trust each student to do so. This requires the instructor to re-

peat reminders such as "do as much as you like." The teacher will soon come to know his or her students and decide which ones need to be encouraged to rest and which ones need to be cajoled into doing more.

3. Touching the students is a good way to help them find the correct way to do the movement. The teacher should be sure to ask for permission. Even though people have agreed to let the teacher manipulate their bodies in some way, it is good to say it aloud before doing it. This can be done simply and directly such as, "I'd like to put my hands on your back while you do the curve. OK? I'm going to touch you all the way down your spine."

4. Demonstrating while doing is necessary. Some older people cannot hear and will simply follow what the teacher does. This is a skill to develop, as it is difficult to demonstrate, keep attention on the students, explain any additional information verbally, and be planning the next step of class.

5. The teacher should walk through the entire space whenever it is possible and continue to demonstrate and verbalize while making eye contact with the students around the circle. Staying on the chair will focus attention on the teacher, but a different kind of contact is often needed to get some of the older people to try the dance. The instructor can walk towards someone and stand in front of him or her. Repeating the movement while this person does it sitting, will be encouraging. This is a very effective way to get some people to dance.

THE WARM-UP: A GENERAL DESCRIPTION

The following warm-up is structured so that the major joints are attended to through a movement exercise. The sequence done while sitting on chairs is basically the same each class. Although they are successful, these exercises are not the only ones that can be done for each joint. In fact, there are many movement possibilities.

When I first began to teach older adults, I started the class with large slow stretch movements of the arms and torso, much in the manner of traditional modern dance classes. One of the elderly students complained of a "bad" shoulder. She said it hurt too much to move her arm upwards. The class stopped and shifted the exercise to just circling the shoulder joint. After a few minutes she was ready to participate in the large warm-ups. That experience taught the author to think about joints first.

Although the warm-up begins with the joints, most of the following descriptions are discussed in terms of peripheral action. Thus, to circle the shoulder, one places the hands on the shoulder but circles the elbows. This creates less stress in the joint while still allowing for the necessary movement. Another example called knee lift is really for the hip joint. To increase the range of movement in that area with as much ease as possible, it is more useful to talk of lifting the knee. If a teacher designs different exercises for the joints, it is good to keep in mind the idea of peripheral action.

Ability to pick up movement quickly is a commodity that younger dancers are supposed to acquire. This is attained by learning a new warm-up in each class and by performing fast recombinations of movement. For older dancers, it may be more important to present structure and security by repeating the same warm-up each week. This way people know they can accomplish at least the beginning part of class. However, some variety is nice, and a creative exploration of some new warm-ups is useful for both teacher and student.

The descriptions that follow use generally accepted language to describe parts of the body. This is not always the correct terminology, but the one that most people will understand. An example is to refer to the abdomen as the stomach.

Breathing

Description: Put your hands on your stomach. Take a deep breath and feel the expanding pressure on your hands. Now let the breath out slowly with a *shhh* sound. See how long you can make the exhale.

Development:
  a. Try it with a loud sigh. Then a louder sound.
  b. Try it with a *ha ha* sound so that the breath is broken up.
  c. Try it with four loud *ha* sounds and four whispered *ha* sounds. Then two of each. Then one of each.
  d. See whose breath can last the longest.

Comments: Try to get people relaxed about feeling overweight. Suggest that it does not matter how big their stomachs are.
Sometimes the breathing makes people cough. Mention that it is OK to cough in class.

Expectations: People might be embarrassed to make the sounds. Try talking about it as a matter of strength. "Let me hear how strong your voices can be." People will laugh.

Figure 1. Thelma ready to begin class with breathing.

— *Head*

Description:	Take your eyes up to the ceiling and let your whole head follow. Then look down. Do not go too fast. Now try looking from side to side. Keep your eyes open and look at the person next to you.
Development:	Take your ear towards your shoulder. Go to the other side. Do not cheat by lifting the shoulder.
Comments:	This provides a good opportunity to help people individually. Gently place your hand by the student's ears and lead them carefully.
	People expect to push hard when they exercise. Caution against this violent approach. In the development version, the weight of the head is used to do the stretch, which allows a more passive approach to the movement.
Expectations:	People might complain of a pain. Sometimes encouraging them to say "ouch" will make them laugh. This releases some tension, and keeps the teacher in touch with what is happening in their bodies. Some will try to do this head movement very hard and very fast. Encourage them to do it softly and slowly.

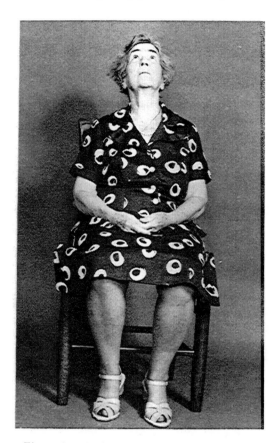

Figure 2. Ada showing head exercises, head up.

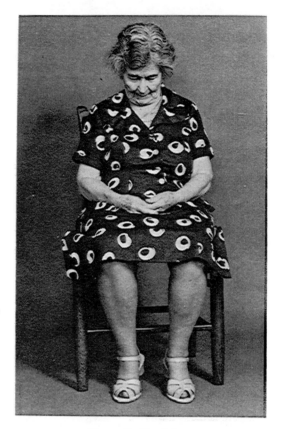

Figure 3. Head down.

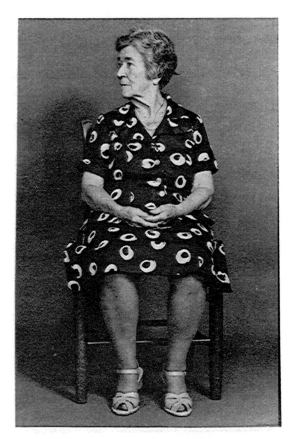

Figure 4. Head to side.

Head/Torso

Description: This movement involves the entire torso. Feel the sit bones on the chair, and imagine a flashlight on the top of the head. Let the light make small circles on the ceiling. This will allow the whole torso to make slow circles. Reverse directions.

Development: The circles get larger.

Comments: People tend to break the head and the torso into two segments. Try to get them to keep it all in one piece.

Expectations: People will enjoy this. They might say that it relaxes them so much that they could go to sleep.

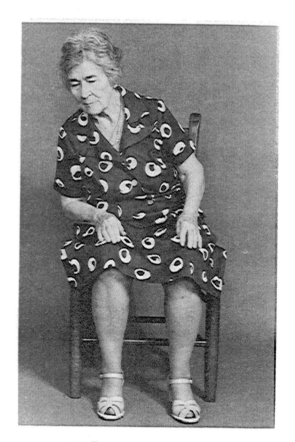

Figure 5. Ada shows head/torso.

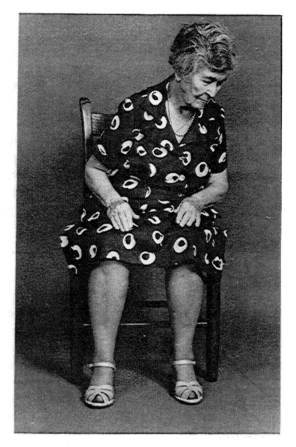

Figure 6. Ada shows head/torso.

Shoulder Lift

Description: Lift shoulders up by your ears, and then release them down easily.

Development: a. Lift just one shoulder up. Lift the other. Alternate.

b. Continue alternating the shoulder lift, but do it more quickly.

c. Lift both up and keep them up for three counts. Bring them down on count four. Repeat, but bring them down on count three. Repeat and bring them down on count two. Then lift them up and down on one count.

d. Combine all the steps of variation c. The pattern then becomes —

up, two, three, down four
up, two, down three
up, down two
up and down

Comments: Remind people to rest. When people lower their shoulders, try not to let them exaggerate the movements so the entire torso collapses. Remind them that this is a shoulder isolation.

Expectations: People will laugh at their mistakes in development step d. Over time they will get the combinations. This is a useful time for the teacher to leave the chair and demonstrate directly in front of people who are not participating. Often they will join this if encouraged.

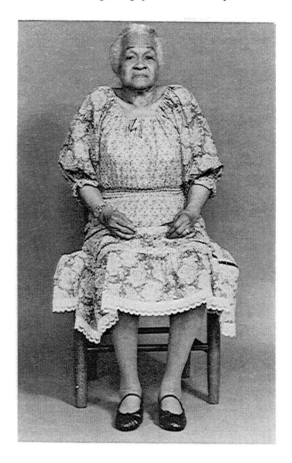

Figure 7. Both shoulders up.

Figure 8. One shoulder up.

Shoulder Circles

Description: Place your hands on top of your shoulders. Circle the elbows. Now change direction.

Development: a. Place your elbows together in front. Now try to put them together behind.

b. What else can move in circles? Solicit ideas from the group.

Comments: Although this exercise is about shoulder circles, stress the movement of the elbow. That way, activity can happen without grinding in the joint.

Expectations: People will have a strong kinesthetic response to this exercise and comment about it. Also, they can tire quickly, so remind them not to overdo. On development step a they will laugh about the attempt to touch the elbows together behind the torso. Some may need to be told that no one can succeed at that, except perhaps a contortionist.

Figure 9. Hands placed on top of shoulders in preparation for shoulder circles.

Figure 10. Elbows touch together in front.

Fingers

Description: Make a fist with fingers closed, then stretch them out. Repeat.

Development: a. Vary the tempo.

b. Do one finger at a time until the whole hand is open. Repeat coming back to a fist, one finger at a time.

Comments: Describe the movement as a flower opening.

Expectations: Not everyone has the dexterity to do the isolations. Often the room is filled with a lot of waving fingers or piano players.

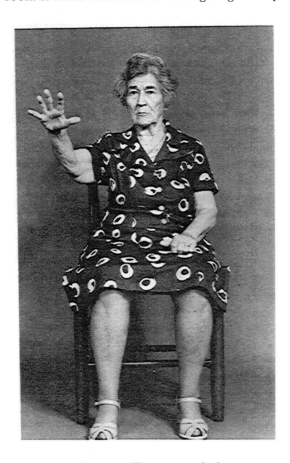

Figure 11. Fingers stretched.

Figure 12. One finger at a time.

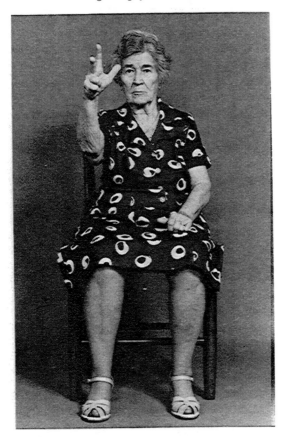

Figure 13. One more at a time.

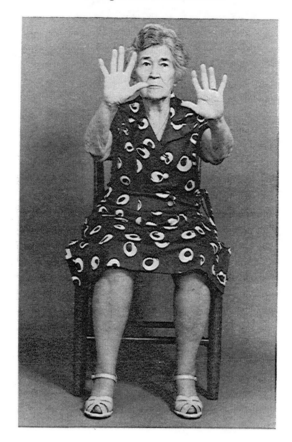

Figure 14. Both hands, fingers stretched.

Hand/Arm Reach

Description: Place hands in loose fists at center of torso. Lift your hands up into the air, reaching with your fingers. Return the hands to the beginning position.

Development: a. Do it forward.
                   b. Do it down, alongside the chair.
                   c. Do it with both arms or one at a time.

Comments: In their enthusiasm people can lose sight of the people around them, so remind them not to hit someone sitting near them. Sometimes people experience pain in their shoulders when they take their arms upwards in the air. Encourage gentleness. Say it is alright to take the arm only part way up.

Expectations: This large movement is one everyone will want to do. Be prepared for a wide variation of movement range. It is not important to have a unified appearance in class. Some people's up direction may look somewhat to the side because their range is so limited.

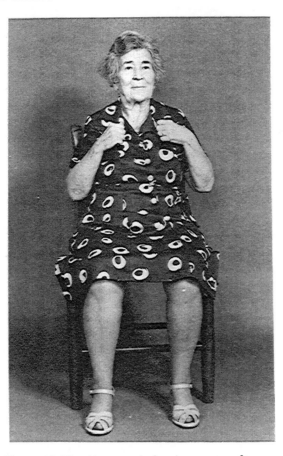

Figure 15. Hand/arm reach, hands at center of torso.

Figure 16. Hands reach up.

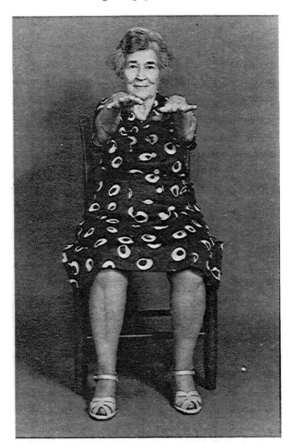

Figure 17. Hands reach forward.

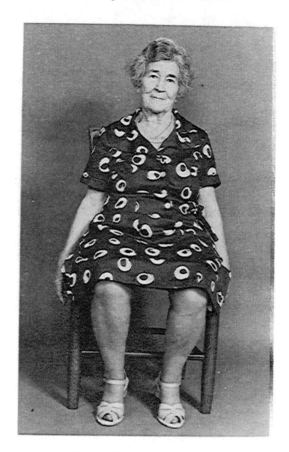

Figure 18. Hands reach down.

Arm Circle

Description: Reach arm down at side. Let the fingers lead the direction of the arm as it circles forward, up and around to the back, and down at side.

Development: This can be combined with the hand/arm reach into a dance phrase. Begin with the hands in the opening position of the hand/arm exercise. Counts one and two: reach hands up and return to opening position. Counts three and four: reach hands forward and return. Count five: reach arm down at side. Counts six, seven, and eight: circle the arm around.

Comments: Let the fingers lead the action. This puts less stress on the shoulder and allows for range in the movement.

It is not necessary for the arm to reach far behind the student. Often the circle becomes more of a side movement than back, which is acceptable.

Expectations: People might hit each other if the chairs are too close together. Ask them to spread out a little or warn them to watch out for their neighbors.

Build a Phrase

Description: Begin by taking both hands into the air above the head and say, "One." This is the first count of the phrase. Then ask someone to do something with his or her arms, and that will be the next count. Look around for an idea presented by one of the students. For example, someone may clap his or her hands above the head. Respond positively and go back to the beginning. Now everyone counts, "And one." The arms go up; on "Two" everyone claps. Look for count three. Someone brings his or her hands to touch the top of the head. Everyone does it. Back to the beginning again. This goes on as long as the teacher and class want to sustain it. Usually eight counts is adequate.

Development: a. Treat it like a theme and variation (see Chapter 6), and try different variations.

b. Remember the arm pattern, and when people are standing later in class, do it while walking around.

c. Choreograph it around a theme. At a holiday time it can be a Thanksgiving phrase or whatever holiday is appropriate, and all the movements can be about that.

d. Add torso and legs as movement choices.

Comment: This is the first less-structured movement in class. The idea is basic to many other improvisations. It is good to get people comfortable with the more open structure while still sitting. Sometimes it takes a while for a group to understand the collec-

tive process or the ways to initiate movement. People will not
give ideas readily.

Just look around and copy someone's natural movements, such
as scratching the head or crossing the arms.

Expectations: This becomes a favorite time in class. People like to give their
ideas and enjoy the complexity of dance. Depending on the
group and the frequency with which the phrase is repeated, it is
possible for the teacher not to dance the final dance but to
watch. However, most of the time, the students will depend on
the teacher's demonstration.

Very often, the kind of movement offered becomes routine. Try
to find ideas and structures that will keep people exploring the
infinite possibilities of their arms.

Figure 19. Ada and Thelma build a six-count phrase, count one.

Figure 20. Count two.

Figure 21. Count three.

Figure 22. Count four.

Figure 23. Count five.

Figure 24. Count six.

Forward Spine Curve

Description: Lead with the top of the head. Softly round forward so that the eyes can see the lap. Slowly continue letting the torso follow the head until the body is as low as it can go without straining. Reverse, bringing the spine up slowly as if putting it against the back of the chair. It is important to leave the head lowered so that it is the last part of the spine to become upright. This is hard to accomplish because the students are used to watching the teacher. In this case they must keep the head, and thus the eye contact, lowered. Pause and repeat.

Comments: This is best done slowly, especially the straightening part. It takes a long time for people to understand how to leave their head curved over. Most will want to pick it up first, which can cause strain in the neck.

This is one of the few exercises in which there is a right and wrong way to perform. Therefore, it is helpful if the students watch once without joining in right away. Sometimes, if you are sure they can hear you, it is helpful to demonstrate the correct and incorrect way to do this. Be sure to exaggerate the incorrect way to hold the head and speak loudly, or they will imitate the wrong way. This is a good time to help the students through touching. It especially helps them to understand keeping the head lowered until the end of the straightening if the teacher uses his or her hands to help them feel the correct way.

Expectations: Some people might complain of dizziness when they first do this. Just tell them to go slowly and perhaps to do it only one time. This subsides over time.

This movement is quite satisfying because it has so much kinesthetic sensation. It is nice to have people talk about how they feel after they do it.

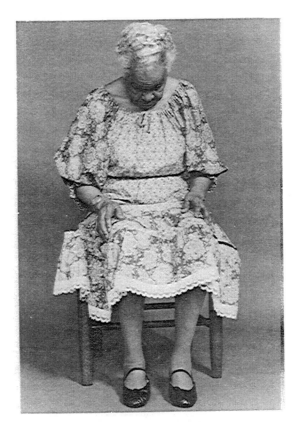

Figure 25. Beginning forward spine curve.

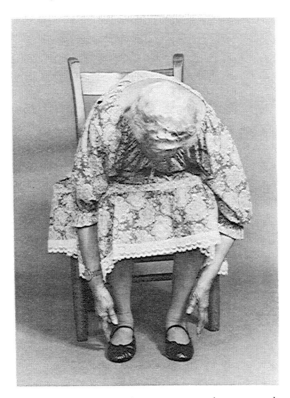

Figure 26. Forward spine curve at maximum stretch.

Figure 27. Teacher shows incorrect use of head in forward spine curve.

Figure 28. Teacher shows incorrect use of head in forward spine curve.

Six-Count Torso

Description: (1) Reach left arm up. (2) Reach right arm toward floor on right side of body. Allow head and torso to curve over to right side. (3) Bring left hand to right hand and clap a few times. (4) Return left arm to up position. (5) Return head to upright (this is aided by thinking of the left arm as reaching higher at the same time). (6) Return left arm to side.

Comments: This is difficult. Do it in classes where people have a lot of energy or seem to need a break in the routine.

Expectations: The difficulty here is in keeping the body in a side low curve at the same time one is actively clapping. Most people will bring their bodies up somewhat.

Figure 29. First of three counts of six-count torso; reach one arm up.

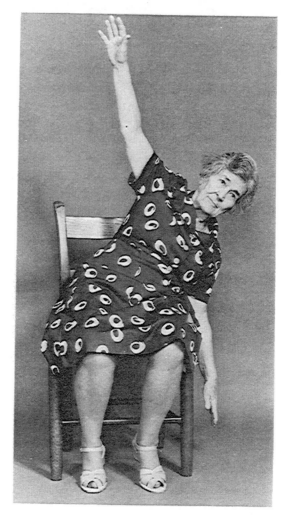

Figure 30. Second count of six-count torso; reach hand toward floor. Let body tilt.

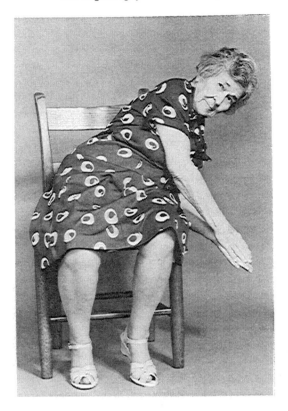

Figure 31. Third count of six-count torso; bring hands together and clap.

Punch w/ Balloon?

Description: Make a fist with the hand, and place at the center of torso. Punch forward with a quick, strong motion. The arm does not have to extend fully. Try not to snap the elbow. Return to center of torso.

Development: a. Do it in different directions.
b. Do it while making an angry face.
c. Occasionally intersperse a quieter, softer arm gesture.

Comments: The sharpness of the gesture is hard for some people. Get them to do it softer and slower. If people do it with angry expressions, often they will laugh.

Expectations: Usually a lot of chatting and quick talking is triggered by this warm-up.

Figure 32. Punch.

Knee Lift

Description: Lift knee up and put it down. Keep the lower leg relaxed. Do not force the torso to remain rigid and upright, but allow it to rock back when the knee is raised and upright when the foot is replaced to the floor. This rocking motion is a result of the movement, so do not force it to happen.

Comment: Look for the correct tempo. Get your cue for this from the older people. Quick is helpful because it is less work on the thigh, though slow is a more comfortable speed for them.

Alternate legs or only do a few at a time on one side to avoid tiring. Only a few repetitions are necessary.

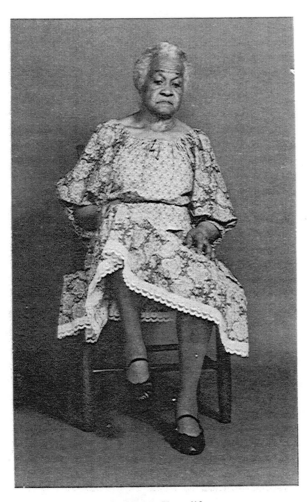

Figure 33. Knee lift.

Leg Stretch

Description: Begin as in knee lift. Raise the knee, then extend the foot forward in the air. Return to the lifted knee position, and replace the foot on the floor. Alternate legs.

Development: a. Add arms. Bring the arms into the center of the torso as the knee is lifted. As the foot extends, take arms forward and up on a high diagonal. Return arms to center and knee to lifted position. Replace foot on floor and arms to side.

b. Same as step a, except keep the leg and arms extended. Let the toes circle in one direction, then reverse. Return as in step a.

Comments: People will tire with too many repetitions. Take a short break and have a discussion about something, or tell stories. Then return to this or a variation, or continue with class.

Expectations: Many people in wheelchairs can do this. Be encouraging to them to try it.

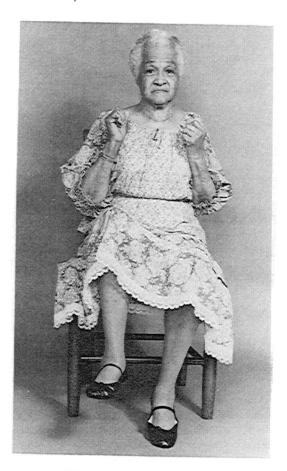

Figure 34. Knee lift with arms.

Figure 35. Leg extended to stretch.

There are many ways to approach foot exercises. The following are several little movements that can be put together in different combinations to make a dance. Two such dances will be described after the various movements are detailed.

Feet I

Description: Begin with feet flat on the floor. Touch toe to floor, then heel, and return the whole foot to the floor.

Comment: It helps to have people say the words *toe, heel, down.*

Expectations: Decide whether it is important that the toe and heel happen in the correct order. If so, it will need practicing. If not, then disregard the different approaches from participants.

Feet II: Brush

Description: Brush the foot along the floor, forward and back. Keep it low.

Comment: Say the words *brush, brush* or *shuffle, shuffle.* (This is in fact a shuffle step from the soft shoe dancing.)

Foot Combination I: Soft Shoe

Description: Touch toe, touch heel, brush forward, brush back, and put the foot down. The rhythm goes (1) toe; (2) heel; (3) brush, brush; (4) down.

Development: a. Ask people for arm or hand movements on each of the counts. Then repeat the dance with just feet, just arms, and combined.

  b. Do with two feet.

Comments: This exercise is fun. This is a nice place to bring in familiar music. This can be worked on over and over. People do not tire of it, and it can be kept challenging by changing the arms.

Expectations: There is a marvelous moment of recognition the first time the dance is completed. They are shocked and delighted at their ability to do it.

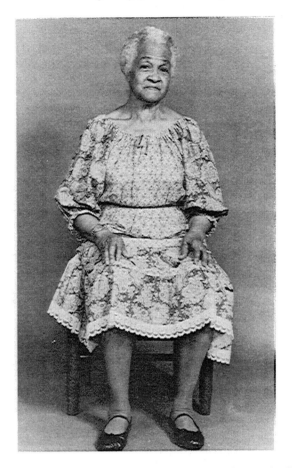

Figure 36. Foot combination I. Begin with both feet on the floor.

Figure 37. Touch toe to floor.

Figure 38. Touch heel to floor.

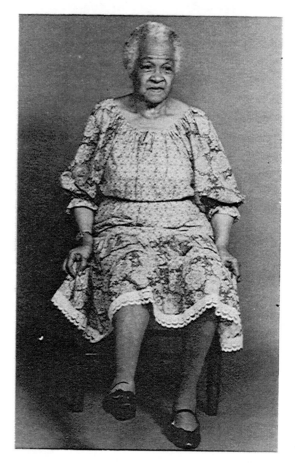

Figure 39. Brush foot against floor and into the air.

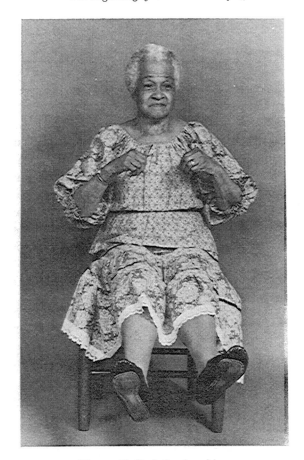

Figure 40. Both feet brushing.

Feet III: Crossings

Description: Cross the ankles. Then open the feet wide apart. Repeat.

Comments: People wearing skirts might complain. Simply tell them not to take their legs so far apart or to do the movement smaller.

Expectations: Some people will lift their legs off the floor. Others will shuffle them along. The teacher must decide on the goal. If it is simply to get people involved and moving to the best of their ability, and that is the first priority, then all the variations are acceptable. If the goal is to teach people specific steps, then the teacher must be very clear in asking for the replication of his or her demonstration. However, many older people will not be able to do the movement exactly for a variety of reasons. Thus, it is best to accept the wonderful attempts and enjoy the differences in people's style and ability.

Feet IV: Practice Jump (While Sitting)

Description: This can be done with the legs close together or wide apart. Push the feet against the floor and spring the legs lightly off the ground a few inches. The whole movement is done quickly, several times in a row.

Comment: The teacher will need to demonstrate. People will catch the rhythm from the teacher.

Expectations: Giggles.

Foot Combination II

Description: This is an eight-count phrase: (1) cross the feet, (2) open the feet wide, (3) cross the feet, (4) open the feet wide, (5) cross the feet, (6) open the feet wide, (7) and (8) three jumps.

Development: a. Do the same thing with the arms. Cross and open them. Clap three times on counts 7 and 8.
   b. Do just the feet or just the arms and then combine.
   c. Reverse so that when the feet are crossed the arms are opened.

Comments: The variation that reverses the arms and feet is difficult to coordinate. People will not get it the first time. There will be many variations, and all are acceptable.

Expectations: People enjoy the kind of confusion that comes from this kind of mixing up of phrases. They also enjoy learning it, so stay with it over several weeks.

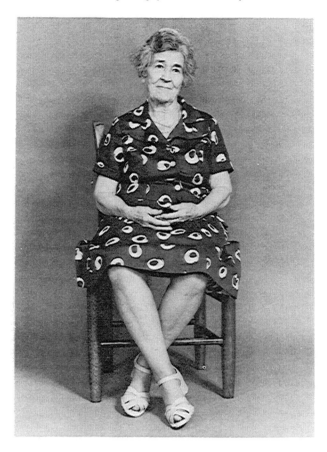

Figure 41. Foot combination II. Feet crossed.

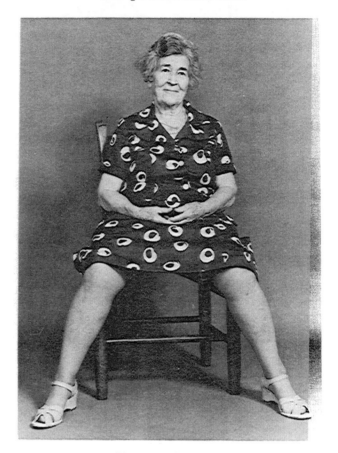

Figure 42. Feet open.

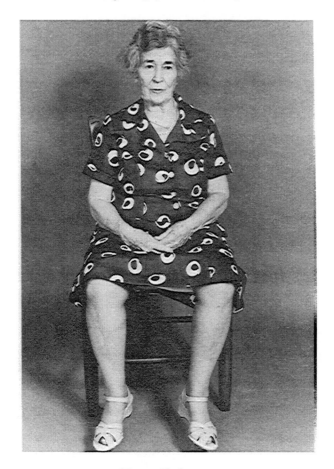

Figure 43. Jump.

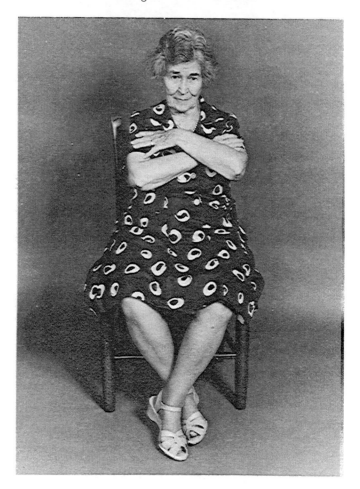

Figure 44. Foot combination II with arms. Feet and arms crossed.

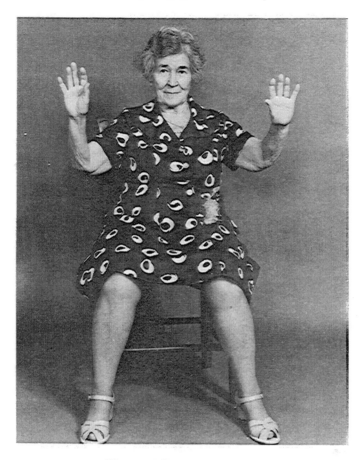

Figure 45. Feet and arms open.

Figure 46. Jump and clap.

Standing Up

Description: This movement begins with a rocking motion, backwards. The torso and head are kept straight (not rigid). Rock backwards and then, with feet flat on the floor and a forward momentum, stand partly up. The torso will rise a few inches from the chair. Count out loud, "One." Then rock back onto the chair, slightly back of center. Repeat. Do a few times, and each rise can be progressively higher off the chair as people learn to control the momentum. Stand on the seventh count.

Comments: This is a good way to get older people to understand how using momentum can be a helpful and easier way to accomplish tasks. This also helps people to learn a way to stand up that does not demand a lot of muscular strength in the thighs.

Expectations: Some people will just rock and stand when everyone else does. Others will work too hard and go to a complete stand each time. Some people will mistakenly rock their head forward and back. If that is all they are doing, it is a good variation. But, if they are attempting to do this while standing up and down, they need to be helped to keep the head straight on the spine. Suggest they keep the torso as one unit.

Carefully watch the people doing this. It is challenging and exciting to succeed at this. For many older people, getting on and off chairs is a major issue. Some will use this ability as a last bastion of self-independence. Thus, they use this warm-up as a kind of challenge: "Of course I can do this." The teacher needs to be aware of this tendency in his or her students. It might be necessary to stand next to someone who wants to try it but who feels tentative or looks tentative and off balance, or whom the teacher suspects to be an overachieving personality.

Chapter Five

STANDING WARM-UPS

NOT everyone in the class will do the standing warm-ups. Not everyone should. The teacher must learn to be comfortable with the student's choice. Most people know their limits and will stand only if they feel safe physically, but again, the need to feel independent, not to acknowledge the change in one's body, might make someone stand up who should not. If that situation arises, the teacher needs to ask the student to sit or to provide an assistant to stand with the older person.

The standing warm-up is all done holding on to the chair. This is not done in the standard ballet position with one hand on the barre. Instead, the students face the chair, holding the back of it with both hands. The teacher must emphasize over and over to hold the chair with both hands. Holding the chairs is done primarily for balance and safety. Some teachers might object to having to be forceful on this issue, perhaps feeling they are treating their students as babies or showing mistrust of their abilities. It cannot be stressed enough how important it is for people to know it is OK to be dependent on the chairs. If people refuse to hold on to the chairs, this section of class will be severely limited.

There are several ways to approach this subject. One is to talk about the ballet tradition and to make sure that everyone has seen pictures of dancers holding the barre. The second is for the teacher to say that it is important for his or her sense of security that the pupils hold on. The only way the teacher can proceed to teach is with the knowledge that people will not fall down.

The teacher must demonstrate holding on, as well. If he or she leaves his or her chair and demonstrates in the middle of the room, many of the older people will drop their hands and do it exactly as their teacher does. Constant verbal and visual reminders are necessary.

Assistants are very helpful for this section of class. If none are available, then the teacher should only do the exercises that make sense to him or her, ones that can be done by rote. This allows for the teacher's total attention to be directed to the group's safety.

The teacher can assign an assistant to a particular older person whom he or she thinks might need help. The assistant can stand next to the senior and also hold a chair. It is important that the assistant participate in class in a normal way. In some exercises the teacher or the assistant can gently place his or her hand on the small of the back of the senior adult. This provides support and a sense of security for the students but does not interfere with their ability to move.

Some of the following exercises are adapted from the ballet tradition. Therefore, their proper dance name is given. Use these terms if it feels comfortable, but it is definitely not a requirement for a good dance class. What is fun, however, is that these terms are recognized worldwide, so the senior dancers who are familiar with this language become part of a large dance community.

Bend and Rise (Plié and Relevé)

Description: Place the feet with toes straight ahead and several inches in between. Bend the knees slowly, and then straighten up. Think of the knees going forward in space as you bend, allowing a small fold in the hip joint and the ankle joint. As you straighten, think about the top of the head leading you up. Do this bend (plié) four times. For the rise (relevé), slowly rise onto the ball of the foot, making sure to keep the hands on the back of the chair. Slowly lower heels to the floor. Do this four times.

Development: a. Turn feet out slightly, keeping the heels either touching or close together. Do four bends (pliés) and rises (relevés) in this position, making sure the knees go over the feet. Think of taking the knees to the side, still folding in the hip and ankle joints.

b. Take the feet wider apart, allowing for six to ten inches of separation. Repeat. Here it is very important to make sure that the knees go over the feet. Students will have a tendency to allow the knees to roll inward. Help them individually.

Comments: Make sure people do not jerk up and down. Use an image to keep it slow, such as "stretch like taffy pulling." It is useful here to demonstrate and exaggerate the way it looks when someone really pushes hard and chops up the movement.

It is not important how deep the student goes in the bend (plié). Some will try to go very close to the floor. Discourage this, as it is very difficult to do correctly. Instead, concentrate on making sure the knees are over the feet no matter what direction the feet are pointing or how wide apart the legs are. Pliés and relevés are part of a long dance tradition. It is fun to give the students background so that they can feel a part of a tradition. It is also good to show them how these exercises relate to dance. Pliés and relevés provide that opportunity, since they form the basis of so many other dance steps.

Expectations: Since this is the first movement done standing up, many people in their chairs will try to come up with a variation. Encourage this, and watch for it during the rest of class.

Figure 47. Rise with hands on chair.

Lunges or Side-to-Side Shifts

Description: The legs are six to ten inches apart. Feet are placed in a comfortable position, neither facing directly forward nor turned out too much to the side. Bend one knee and then the other. This allows the weight to shift from one leg to the other.

Development: a. Let the head begin to lead the body, still bending one knee. It should be done in a relaxing manner. When the head is leading, the student can still think of the knee. Remember to think of the knee going over the foot.
  b. Add a plié. Bend one knee, then both, then the other, and straighten both. This makes a circular motion.
  c. Add an arm on the lean. If one leans to the right, the left arm (upper) reaches over the head in the direction of the lean.

Comments: It does not matter which way people lean first. Some will mirror the teacher, and some will go opposite.

Expectations: There will be confusion at first. People will think they are wrong, since invariably someone will go to a different side. Sometimes there are collisions, which cause little fights, raised voices, and good-humored response. Saying "left" and "right" does not seem to help the situation. People might make mistakes about which is right and left, which only adds to the embarrassment.

It is nice to use an image such as waving wheat. I like to talk about the Wisconsin farms I used to see in my childhood. The seniors appreciate the feeling, the image, and the story.

Twists

Description: Keep one hand on the chair. Lift the other arm straight in front, at shoulder height. Bring the arm across the body. Then open the arm away to the back. Think of the hand painting a wide circle. Let the eyes (focus) follow the hand. Go as far as you can and then come back. Change arms and repeat to the other side.

Comments: Try to get people to understand crossing the body and opening away from the body. This helps solve the left-right issue.

Expectations: People will probably hit each other. Try to prepare them for this by saying, "Keep your eyes open so you don't hit your neighbor." People will have trouble with the cross-open idea. Instead, they will mirror the teacher, which might mean as you are saying, "Go as far as you can" (open), they are in the closed position. It can be frustrating. People will also let go of the chair. Remind them to keep one hand on the chair back.

Figure 48. Twist, arms across body.

Figure 49. Twist, arm opening.

Foot Tap (Tendu)

Description: Align feet straight ahead. Place the ball of the foot forward, on the floor under the chair, and then replace it in standing position. Repeat four times. Then do the other foot.

Development:
a. Do it to the side.
b. Do it to the back.
c. Combine. Do it front, side, back, and return to standing position. Alternate feet.

Comments: This is not a strict tendu. They emphasize brushing the foot on the floor. This is more of a tap.

It is sometimes difficult for people to catch on to development step c. It helps to have people say the words *front, side, back,* and *in* on a rhythm duplicating what will be done with the feet. Then combine words and movement.

This is a good place for bright, lively music.

Expectations: This feels complicated, and people will enjoy their accomplishments. This is a good place to encourage the people sitting in their chairs to follow along.

Figure 50. Foot tap forward.

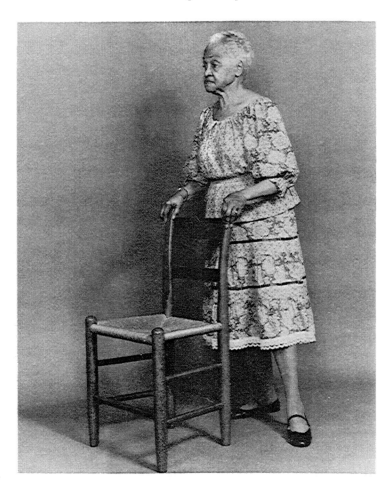

Figure 51. Foot tap to side.

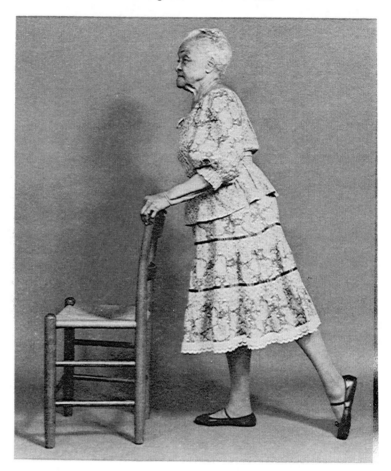

Figure 52. Foot tap back.

Knee Lift (Passé)

Description: Stand with heels together, feet slightly turned out. Bring the toe of the foot to the side of the opposite knee. Replace the foot. Do four times and go to other side.

Development: Bring the toe to the knee on count one. Stretch the toe out to the side (diagonally between front and side) on count two. On three return the foot to the knee, and on four replace the foot to standing position.

Comments: Because students are facing the chairs, it is possible to bring the knee forward up and hit the chair. Demonstrate this first, in an exaggerated manner. Then show how to avoid this by keeping the leg slightly turned out. That position not only corrects the collision problem but is in fact a logical development from the position of the feet. Use the words *up, out, in, down* in a rhythm for the development. It is hard to find the right tempo for this. A slow rate is easier to do, except that the balance is harder. Quick is exciting, except that people tend to throw their legs too hard. Work to find a balance. Try using a four-count rhythm for the movement, and then a four-count rest. Alternate legs.

Expectations: Watch to see which leg people use. Some will mirror the teacher, and some will do the right side first. There are almost always collisions.

Figure 53. Knee lift (passé).

Figure 54. Leg extension for knee lift.

The following three stand-up exercises should be done with great care. Wait until you know your students well and can help determine who should do what. Be sure to have plenty of assistants to help, or watch one student do them at a time. They are presented here in order of complexity and difficulty.

Arabesque

Description: Begin in a standing position. Feet can be forward or slightly turned out. Touch the toe back as in the back tendu. Then slowly lift the leg off the floor. Allow the torso to come forward in order to balance. This will also prevent the back from pinching. Bring the foot back to the tendu position and then replace the foot to standing.

Development: When the leg is in the air behind the student, let one arm come off the chair, and reach forward in space. Return the arm and then the leg. Make sure that one hand is always on the chair.

Comment: Hold the arabesque briefly, for about three counts. Make sure the body is forward; otherwise, it is easy to pinch the back.

It is logical to ask, Why do this exercise? One answer is that many people associate ballet with an arabesque. It brings great pleasure to the older dancers to do this, to be told about its traditions, and to accomplish what they regard as a real dance step.

Expectations: Frustration from some, with comments such as "She expects us to do *that.*" This comes with an accompanying grunt, or sigh, or disapproval. Sometimes this happens with any movement, but it is especially noticeable with these difficult ones. Encourage those who are not doing it to enjoy watching the others. Show them how difficult it is to accomplish, even for the teacher. Have them practice the arm movement with it in their chairs.

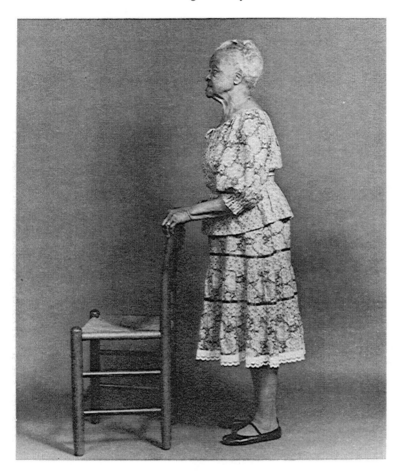

Figure 55. Standing position ready to move.

Figure 56. Arabesque.

Jumps

Description: Begin with a slow bend, rise, and bend that are connected, with no stop in between. This is a slow-motion jump. Make sure that people understand the plié at the end. Bend the knees, keep hands on the chair, and do a quick, light jump into the air. Stop after one.

Development: a. Demonstrate two quick jumps. Then have the class follow. Repeat up to four times.

b. Do three jumps. On the fourth, land with the legs farther apart (six to ten inches), and on the fifth return to the starting position.

Comments: Remind people to keep their hands on the chairs. This is a slightly awkward position to jump in. People will have to bend a little forward.

Remind them not to push down on the chair as they go into the air, as sometimes the chairs have a tendency to slip. Instead, rest the hands lightly. Remind people that they can do the slow-motion jump instead of the quick one.

Expectations: Applause.

Figure 57. Jess jumps still holding chair.
PHOTO: DeLoria

Forward Spine Curve: Standing

Description: This is similar to curving the spine while sitting. Have people lower their heads and then begin curving over the chair. Let the hands slide down the side of the chair so that one is always in contact with it. Slowly return to upright with the head being the last part of the body to be straight.

Development: Curve over the chair. Place hands on the chair and bend the elbows to the side and then straighten. This is like a push-up. It can be done several times. Then return to upright.

Comments: The back can uncurl without using effort in the arms. Some people might feel too weak to do this, so they will "climb" back up by using the side of the chair. This is OK, but watch that the chair does not slip out from under them.

Expectations: Dizziness. Go slowly and repeat only twice. Have lots of support. Encourage partnering by assistants.

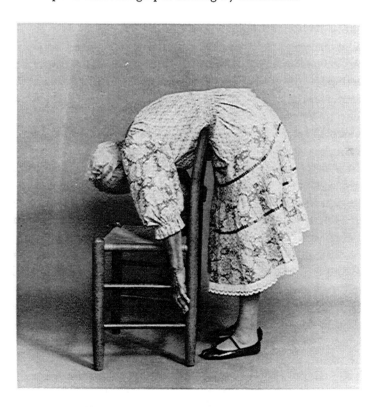

Figure 58. Forward spine curve, standing.

Chapter Six

MOVING INTO THE CENTER:
IMPROVISATION

IT is time for the students to dance more fully, and this means away from the chairs. The class is designed to get progressively more demanding, so fewer people might actively participate as the class proceeds.

Those who choose not to move to the center can continue to enjoy the class by watching, encouraging others, or continuing to adapt the standing work to movements done while sitting. At this time, those who are willing join in a circle in the center of the room. It may be necessary to take time to push chairs back a little to make more room.

It is fine to take several moments for this transition. Some students stop and discuss whether to participate further. Some need to be persuaded by the teacher or other students to participate. It is important to distinguish the possible responses to this next activity and to act accordingly.

One type of student might be embarrassed or afraid of incompetence. These people need to be encouraged and supported in whatever way possible to join: "Come on, sure you can do it. Give it a try." These are phrases that can help. This is very difficult for some younger teachers to do. They feel that this begging or bullying is awkward. It is, however, necessary, and after one knows the students well, it is easy to find the right ways to encourage participation.

Some students are limited in activity because of deteriorating health. They like the class and do all the movements in the chair. At this point they are uncertain whether to continue or not. Talk to them. Perhaps they can stand in the center for a while. Perhaps the teacher, assistant, or other student can hold their hands the entire time they are standing. This is a place where the teacher must be comfortable with the decision. It may be necessary to tell the student not to participate or to take several minutes later in the class with them alone so that safety is insured.

Improvisation

The standing work emphasizes improvisation, which is a way of dancing freely within a directed structure. Some structures are fairly limiting, such as doing a happy dance with hands only. Other structures can be very open, such as dancing to the music. There are uses for each kind of improvisation. To limit the possibilities is not bad. In fact, some people need to be limited so that making choices is possible. Others thrive in completely open improvisational structures. The teacher can try many different structures to find which ones the class responds to with the most ease and which ones require help from him or her.

Why Improvisation?

The beauty of improvisation for the elderly is that it can free people to dance for a long period of time without having to remember steps. It can be a solo or group activity, allowing for contact with each other, but is not frustrating the way learning a group routine can be. The improvisation can be beautiful and fulfilling for participants and fun to watch for those on the side. It can be structured to relate directly to the mood of the class or the needs of the students at any particular moment. If people need to slow down or be quiet, the improvisation can reflect that. If some are ready to be very active and others not, it can be structured in two parts so that each can do what is appropriate to them. It can also free imaginations. One of the most beautiful improvisations I have seen consisted of a woman walking gently around the room, moving her arms and talking softly about a trip to the park. Her imagination was alive with the exact trees she saw, the color of the birds, the smell of the small flowers, and the quiet of the wispy clouds. Externally, visually, she looked only as if she were walking in circles in the Roosevelt, but for those within hearing distance, and for herself, she was transported.

Rules for Improvisation

There are only three rules for all improvisations. First, it is impossible to be wrong, to make a mistake. Anything a student does is fine. Second, a student may not hurt herself or himself on purpose. This means taking care to sit down when tired and being sure not to let the movement structure of the improvisation allow for self-destruction. Last, no one can, on purpose, hurt anyone else. The latter two rules use the words *on purpose.* Sometimes in improvisation there can be accidents. A dancer might fall or bump into someone else, which can lead to injury. This has never happened in a Dance Exchange class for older dancers, but a teacher should be aware of the potential for this.

Improvisation presents many challenges for the teacher. It is important to remain uninvolved in the improvisation in order to observe the action and to see how to direct the students further. This also means watching for potential problems and stepping in to support someone if necessary. However, this is not a rigid process. Sometimes it is best to coach by moving among the dancers, talking and demonstrating, giving ideas verbally and physically. Usually a teacher will find himself or herself doing some of both: dancing for a few moments and then stopping to watch and make room for others.

The improvisation session might begin thirty-five minutes into the class. Some students may have tired. Others have chosen not to stand or cannot participate in so active a dance. Therefore, there are probably many people watching. Usually, the participants are so involved that this will not disturb them, but it is helpful to reiterate occasionally that improvisation is for the dancer, not the audience. There are times when the class may choose to perform the improvisations. At that time, it is for the audience and is danced accordingly, but improvisations themselves begin with the dancer and are for that person, whether he or she is looking for self-expression, new movement ideas, fun, or contact with a group.

Holding Hands in the Center

Very often the standing group will begin in a circle. Holding hands is a natural way to keep contact with each other and to maintain balance. Occasionally, a student may not want to hold someone's hand. Each teacher must solve this in an appropriate way. Usually the reason for not wanting to hold another's hand is prejudice. One member of the Roosevelt group does not like to hold the hand of people who are a different race or slightly disabled. This is unacceptable behavior. She is asked to hold hands or to leave the circle. It does no good to coddle any person's prejudice. It is important to respect the older person's ideas and feelings but not to support behavior that is unacceptable in any other situation.

The Ritual of Introductions

The first dance done standing is called "solo dance introductions." It may take several weeks or even months for people to become totally comfortable with this format, but in time, people come to cherish it as a time to oversee each other's progress and enjoy the experience of a solo dance.

Given the nature of a class with its changing population and the probability that some memories might be vague, it is helpful to repeat names each week. It is also affirming to make dances from such a basic element as our names. (In a class where over half of the students do not join the standing section, it is good to do introductions earlier, while in the chairs, and to repeat them standing with the smaller group.)

There are many ways to do this. The basic one is simply to go around the circle and have each person say his or her name. Then, do it again and add movement structures to go with the introduction. Following are several ideas for this:

1. Say your name and do a dance. Any dance is fine. It can be modified by doing a dance about your day, about the way you are feeling, about a theme that might be further developed in later improvisations.
2. Say your name and just take a shape with your body, like sculptures.
3. Say your name, walk into the center, take a shape with your body, and dance back to your place.

Some of the people who join the circle normally use a walker or occasionally a wheelchair. Therefore, it is good for those in the circle to hold hands while people dance their introductions in the center. This will help all keep their balance. If the group is a very active one and the teacher feels confident about the safety of the students, it is sometimes nice for all to copy the movement or shape of each dancer. Repeating the name of the dancer while she or he is performing is another variation.

New students to the class, or people who are quite scared or inhibited, might have trouble just getting up and dancing freely. They will say something such as, "I can't do this, I don't know what to do." First, the instructor should try being supportive and say, "Sure you can," or, "Just listen to the music and dance a little." Many of the other students will probably offer prompting from the side with comments such as, "Just waltz a little," or "Move your arms around." It may be necessary to quiet them in order to let the new student have time to think. Sometimes, though, these coaching ideas are helpful.

If students are still reluctant, the teacher should try taking their hands and dancing together. Some will require the teacher to lead them entirely. Others, once they sense the instructor's presence, will take over and lead the duet. It is good for the teacher to be as neutral as possible when dancing with a student at this time so that the student can recognize his or her own power in the situation.

The author has witnessed extraordinary transformations in new students as they realize that the teacher is there for support and that they can direct the movement. Within half a minute they begin to build strength in their dancing, joy in their faces, and immense delight in being part of the process.

Students will come to feel very supported in the circle and, consequently, quite safe. Occasionally their exuberance, freedom, and the fun of the moment will make them try dances that they cannot always control. For example, one woman once decided to start spinning. She did beautifully the first two times but was unable to control the dizziness that comes naturally with this movement. This woman did not fall, but she did need the arm of the teacher on her third spin. Therefore, the teacher stands in the circle in order to catch a fall or provide support for a slight imbalance. This is a difficult role to play, since one does not want to inhibit the participation. Like the spinning woman, however, others might need the very sudden help of the teacher. Usually, in this situation, the teacher can direct attention to the dancing students and follow them in the circle as they dance, like a shadow, giving them plenty of room to experiment.

Having an additional person in the center while the people dance might cause a conflict for the teacher, since he or she may also have to stand in the circle in order to hold someone's hand for balance. Therefore, during the transition time in class, when people are deciding to join the circle, the teacher needs to make a quick assessment of the class's strength for that evening. Based on the number of assistants, or strong students, he or she may determine that not everyone should stand. This is not a rigid decision. It changes from week to week, depending on who is there.

Often these classes are attended by family members, interested dancers, or practitioners from the field. Encourage them or any visitor to participate in the circle. Staff who may just be passing by can also join the circle briefly. They, too, might be momentarily embarrassed, but it is a remarkable moment of democracy as everyone gets their turn to perform.

It is nice to have music for these introductions, although it is not essential. The teacher might play one record that has dynamic changes in it so that people can respond differently. The problem with prerecorded music is that the introductions are designed to allow all students to dance completely on their own terms. Music will definitely affect their choice. A sensitive accompanist is best, since he or she will be able to support these individual dances beautifully.

OVERVIEW OF IMPROVISATIONAL TECHNIQUES AND MATERIAL

The remainder of this chapter is divided into two parts. The first is a series of techniques for improvisation. Bare structures are provided that can work with pure movement or with thematic ideas. The second section is devoted to finding material or content for the improvisation. It will show how to get ideas for themes, how to generate excitement, how to make it important enough to the dancers to move within the provided structures. Theoretically, every thematic idea can be done within each structure.

Techniques	**Finding Material for Improvisation**
Build a phrase	Memories
Follow the leader	Holidays
Theme and variation	Stories
Mirroring	Feelings
Sculptures	Everyday activities
Isolations	Seasons
Pass the dance around	Environments
Word dances	Images
Be the word	Poetry
Be a person with the word	Music
Be an environment in which	Pure movement
the word would be a part	
How would you be if	

Some improvisations are better done as solos, and some in pairs. Others are best done in circles or lines. Some use the whole room, others use just the center area or the chairs. It is important to be as open and creative with the structures as possible.

The students will be sending cues all the time. The teacher should watch and listen to them as they dance. Sometimes a word muttered under the breath is the appropriate thing to say next or to try with a group. The teacher should not hesitate to let a student give ideas.

Improvisational Techniques

BUILD A PHRASE: As already described in the chapter on chair warm-ups, building a phrase is the compilation of movement ideas taken from individuals in the class. The exercise begins with one movement and then others are added. Each time a movement is added, the class should go back to the beginning and repeat the sequence. Movements can be short one-count ideas or longer passages requiring a change of rhythm.

FOLLOW THE LEADER: Follow the leader is an adaptation of the game people played as children. Here, however, the teacher calls out who leads, and everyone follows. It can be decided in advance how accurate the followers have to be. Directions can be given to use particular body parts, that is, just the arms or elbows. In that case everyone follows that specific idea. It is also possible for whoever is leading to call out the next leader.

THEME AND VARIATION: Theme and variation requires a phrase that everyone already knows. It can be one made by building a collective eight-count dance that everyone has just learned. It could be something the class has been working on for a while. The class is asked to find ways to vary the movement, keeping the sequence in order. Once a movement phrase is learned, there are myriad ways to vary it. Since movement is done in space, with a sense of timing and energy, it is useful to think of variations within these three concepts. One does not necessarily approach the seniors with these ideas of space, time, energy (or dynamics), but if one keeps these options in mind, the variations will flow endlessly. For example, to vary space means to think of where the phrase travels, whether to do it high or low, whether the movement takes much space and is exaggerated or becomes small, isolating to one body part. It is also possible to manipulate tempo and rhythm. Slowing down or speeding up phrases is one of the most satisfying movement variations for the elderly. Energy and dynamics refer to how a movement is done. Adding force or tension to a phrase or doing it softly, as if in water, suggests the potential here.

In addition to these movement variations, a teacher can change the environment. Different music will change the dance. One can add the idea of mood or texture to the air, such as suggesting that students dance as if in a dense fog or wet cement. It is possible to dance the phrase with an emotional state, as if angry or proud. These ideas will produce the same kind of variations

Figure 59. Mirroring.

that come from changing time, space, and rhythm, but for older people or those new to dance, it is sometimes easier to get a response by using images rather than conceptual language.

Theme and variation is an excellent way to learn sequential material. The variations allow the group to repeat the same phrase over and over without getting bored. It is also possible to make a very long dance using the same sequence.

It is not necessary, however, to begin with a routine or counted dance phrase. Theme and variation can be used in a more free-style form. The teacher can play music and let people just dance. One simply calls out the variations, such as, "Move just the arms; go slowly; make sure to go to each corner of the room." The theme can also be part of another improvisational structure. For example, someone could be a tree that is moving gently in the wind. Changing the wind to thunderstorms, to freezing cold, or to any image changes the trees, too.

MIRRORING: In mirroring, one should divide the group into pairs and let one dancer start moving slowly and have the other mirror the movements (Figs. 59, 60, and 61). This means there will be simultaneous movement. It

Figure 60. Mirroring.

may be necessary to demonstrate, since some people will do oppositional movement rather than mirror image. This exercise is important for several reasons.
First, it helps people develop an eye for movement. If one person raises an
arm, the other must raise it the same way the leader does, not do it differently.
Sometimes this is impossible because of body limitations, but this exercise can
teach the older people how to adapt movement immediately to their own
bodies. It is also important for the younger dancers present, who are often
challenged to give movement that their senior partner can do while still dancing in a way that satisfies the self.

SCULPTURES: The sculpture exercise has several steps leading up to the actual improvisation. First, people just make shapes with their bodies. They are
encouraged to find different shapes, to change levels, and to experiment. Then
one person should stand in a comfortable position in the center of the circle.
Another connects to the first person by touching some part of his or her body.
The teacher can add up to seven people. After people are connected, music is
played and everyone moves free style (Fig. 62). When the music stops, they re-
connect to form a new sculpture.

Figure 61. Mirroring.

In the beginning it is important to limit the number of participants in each sculpture. This improvisation takes a few minutes to set up. While some people are connecting to the first sculpture, others have been holding their original positions. This requires strength and endurance, which need to be developed. Also, too many people can crowd the group. Once the free-style dancing begins, it is easy to have collisions. The touching during the sculptures causes laughter and excitement. When the free-style dancing comes, it is usually quite exuberant in response to this energy. The teacher must keep peripheral vision on everything at once and perhaps join the improvisation if it needs his or her physical energy as well. If there is no music available, he or she may want to lead the nonparticipants in a rhythmic clapping to support the free-style moving. An arm signal, or verbal cue, from the teacher will stop this "hand orchestra," and the dancers will freeze.

Those who are not in the sculpture can watch from the circle or sit down and wait for their turn. As the class improvisational skills develop, the number of participants can increase.

ISOLATIONS: The students are asked in the isolations to explore as many

Figure 62. Free-style dancing at the Roosevelt, Ada Welch and Elsie Schreiber.
PHOTO: Reinhard

ways of moving as possible with one part of their bodies. Since the arms are the most mobile of parts for the elderly, many seniors get the most satisfaction from arm dances. But, to dance with just the hips or belly is not only fun but also shows the range of movement still possible in older bodies. Finger and hand dances are wonderful to do for people in chairs, wheelchairs, or even beds. Face dances may cause initial embarrassment, but someone invariably will say, "It's good for you," and many will try it. Leg or feet dances can be done while holding hands or sitting.

PASS THE DANCE AROUND: Pass the dance around is a very basic structure, where one person will dance in the middle and then select someone to replace him or her. Each person gets a turn. This is nice since picking someone is a way to express friendship or to tease someone. Many themes can be combined with this structure.

WORD DANCES: Many structures fit loosely around the use of words. First,

Figure 63. Word dance: Thelma is a person with a kite.
PHOTO: DeLoria

one can be the word. The dancer becomes the object stated, such as a kite. Second, the dancer can be a person in relation to the word. Thus, someone could be flying a kite. Third, the dancer could be part of the environment in which one finds the word, such as being the wind that is blowing a kite. Examples of these are shown in Figures 63 through 66.

This exercise is a very rich structure. Older people seem most comfortable with the structure that allows them to be the person with the word. The problem with this is that very often it does not employ much movement. For example, the person with the kite can stand still, hold the string, and look into the air. However, once one becomes the kite there are a great number of possibilities. The teacher must take a long time exploring this idea with students. For most people, relating to the world with their bodies in a semiabstract way is

Figure 64. Word dance: Judy is the string of the kite.
PHOTO: DeLoria

something they did as children. It is unfortunate that most people stopped then, because there is much to be gained by this form of movement exploration. When people become objects other than themselves they are freed to feel and act differently. They allow themselves to think in totally new ways, which can be a very liberating experience. This process brings mind and body together in a unique way, helping them to imagine, to create, and to initiate change. For older people this is a powerful and important moment.

Of course, people are not objects other than themselves and for some older people this is a very difficult concept to grasp. Many of them have spent their lives in very realistic patterns. They have not been involved in the arts or been active creating in their imaginations. For some, this is the most difficult part of dance class. They can be the person playing with the kite, but they cannot be the kite because they are not the kite. Yet, to get them to try this, experience

Figure 65. Word dance: Vee is the wind.
PHOTO: DeLoria

this, is very important. The teacher should expect a discussion and perhaps even an argument. It is best to agree with them that they are not the kite and to explain that the idea is to find the quality of the kite, or its essence, and to embody that as a human being. It is important to persevere with these discussions because with the understanding of this concept comes one of the true gifts dancing can bring people. It allows for a very different relationship with the world.

Being something in the environment of the kite is a useful group experience. In this movement exercise people can choose from such things as the wind, the string, clouds, birds, trees, or other kites. Listening to the choices people make can be as much fun as the dance itself, which is usually performed in a free-form style. It is important that people learn they do not have to be literal. The audience of onlookers or other classmates does not have to under-

Figure 66. Word dance: Jess is the kite.
PHOTO: DeLoria

stand the improvisation. Each person is what they say they are.

Occasionally, someone in class will challenge the chosen expression of a dancer. The teacher or another student should reiterate that this is the individual dancer's choice. If the criticism is offered in a useful manner, it is possible to take time to explore other ways to dance the subject at hand, but the main goal is to convince each person of his or her ability to select an idea and move in whatever way he or she wants in relation to that idea.

One person at the Roosevelt always does the same dance, even though the theme changes from week to week. She talks clearly about her different ideas but repeats the same proud prance around the circle each week. The rest of the group accepts this, and the class continues.

HOW WOULD YOU BE IF: How would you be if is a basic structure for improvisations on the chair. Using feeling words, the teacher asks the students how they would sit if they were tired, or happy, or excited. They respond with

Figure 67. How would you be if: bored.

different sitting positions (Figs. 67 through 70). Later these attitudes can be applied to a phrase as a theme and variation. This is a good way to get people used to expressing emotion quickly without having to go very deeply into the feeling. Also, everyone can do it.

Finding Material for Improvisation

The techniques for improvisation may not be enough to satisfy older dancers. They need a reason to dance within these structures besides the fun and good health the movement provides. It is important to add themes, ideas, and substance to the structures so that the hour can be meaningful. The following are sources for ideas. These are just a starting point. There are ideas for dances everywhere.

MEMORIES: Remember a time when you were on the beach, in the mountains, or at a birthday party. Tapping pleasant memories can be a rewarding experience for older people and their teachers. A dance can be made by a

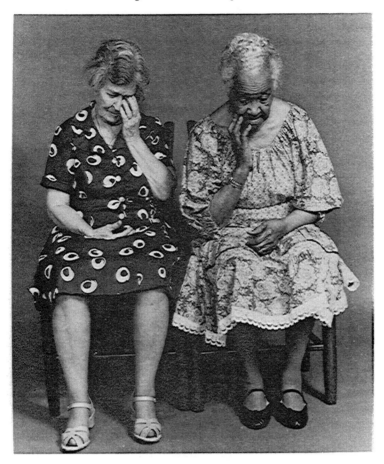

Figure 68. How would you be if: sad.

patchwork of these memories, with different dancers telling stories about the same theme. One could also pick something less personal, such as old movies. People can be encouraged to remember their favorite stars, the trip to the theater, the music that went with it, or the food and then decide which structure will best let these memories come alive.

HOLIDAYS: Holiday themes are a very lucrative area for dances. Holidays are filled with memories, as well as current thoughts. Even though many older people are separated from their loved ones and may have sad feelings about being alone, dancing offers a way to share the experiences of the holiday. Holiday improvisations can include becoming Halloween characters, unwrapping or being Christmas presents, lighting the Chanukah menorah, interpreting fireworks and freedom dances for the Fourth of July, giving slavery and freedom dances at Passover, and eating food, food, and more food.

In fact, food is often on the minds of the older people, especially at a place such as the Roosevelt where mealtimes break the isolation and routine of the day. Almost every improvisation can end with images of food. Any of the struc-

Figure 69. How would you be if: excited.

tures can be used to reflect this imagery. The challenge is to get away from the mimetic action of eating and look for other ways to express the subject.

STORIES: The teacher can collect stories from the class participants or choose a theme if it will help get them going. It might be a holiday theme or a sporting event theme. Sometimes people need a trigger word to get them thinking. Often if a person begins a story about a certain theme, everyone will follow the same theme anyway, unless the teacher gives a different direction. (Once at a workshop, an older person told a disaster story about being on a boat that capsized. Every other person in the room then told disaster stories, at least half of which happened on boats.)

Once the instructor has the story, there are several approaches to take. Eventually one has to find a structure that fits best. That might call for the teacher to narrate it and let people respond. It might be dividing the story up and having people do different parts in different structures, or once the story is told, everyone can do an impression of it. This takes practice and a willingness to experiment. Some structures will work and some will not.

Figure 70. How would you be if: proud.

FEELINGS: Dancing feelings can be a lovely experience for the class. It is threatening for some people to dance about feelings, since the dancing may increase the intensity of the emotion. Some structures, however, are safer than others emotionally. If people do happy dances with their hands rather than their whole body, it is likely to be a different experience. Also, the teacher can direct the class to use the lighter emotions such as joy, happiness, or embarrassment. Figures 71 and 72 illustrate two examples of dances based on feelings.

No one, including the teacher, will venture into intense emotional depths unless he or she feels comfortable doing so. Because of the nature of dance, there are many emotional levels in which a person can be dancing. For example, when asked to do a sad dance, one older person may caricature the feeling, exaggerating to the point that everyone laughs. Another will let herself feel the emotion and does a very touching dance, which makes everyone quiet for a moment.

In rehearsal for the dance *Woman of the Clear Vision*, the older people were asked to dance as dead spirits, welcoming the author's mother to their

Figure 71. Dance based on anger.

world. When asked how they felt performing the dance, they all had different levels of involvement with the imagery. Only one let herself fully experience the dance and its meaning. It took another woman three revivals of the dance over a three-year period finally to stop counting the movement phrase and feel the feelings instead.

That is the beauty of dance — when a person is ready, he or she can connect to the feeling level. If not, counting, or caricaturing, or being funny are all ways to be active, to become part of the group, and to expand the nature of life experience.

Everyday Activity and Work: Finding out what people did during the day can be an interesting base for a dance. The teacher can ask each person to contribute something and then make a composite dance of all the activities. Theme and variation, build a phrase, or word dances will keep it going. Often a single activity will generate plenty of movement ideas. For example, swim-

Figure 72. Dance based on joy.

ming, walking to the store, visiting with a friend, scaring the pigeons, sleeping, dreaming, eating are all possible improvisational activities.

Sometimes people refer to everyday activities that they used to do. Gardening, chopping wood, calisthenics while in the navy can all become subjects for improvisations.

SEASONS: The seasons offer many images for improvisation. One of the wonderful things about improvising with dance is the possibility of going from specific details to moods or feelings. The seasons conjure up images that lend themselves to this kind of improvisational dance. Thanksgiving holiday food, raking leaves, first snows, Halloween characters, and falling leaves can occur side by side depending on the structure. Older people can let their minds settle briefly in passing images or stay with one for a while.

ENVIRONMENTS: Environments are like the seasons in their potential for tiny detail or moods. The instructor should let someone pick a place such as a desert or jungle. People have a wide choice of objects to be, qualities such as the texture of the air, colors, and even sounds from which to choose. The more abstract an improvisation gets, the easier it is for the students to lose touch with what they are doing. The teacher may find it necessary to coach on the sidelines. This means an occasional word or movement to help get them back in touch with the material. Usually they do fine and just need to be reassured that to move abstractly is all right.

A teacher might also want to change structures. In other words, it is important to be flexible. Preplanning is crucial, but the situation may require something else. For example, the students may be improvising on a jungle environment but seem to run out of ideas. The teacher might stop the class and look for a moment at each person's dance, asking each to say what he or she is doing. As a group they could then build a jungle phrase by making a sequence of the individual dances. This might be followed by a follow-the-leader dance around the room with the teacher calling out variations.

IMAGES: Images are pictures in people's minds that everyone can dance to in his or her own way. This concept originally developed at the Roosevelt out of an experience with T'ai Chi, a form of martial art. Rima Wolff, a frequent substitute teacher in the Dance Exchange senior program, does a form of T'ai Chi each time she substitutes at the Roosevelt. Although I do not know the form, I have watched her teach it several times. The students began requesting it even when Rima did not come. I asked them to show me the forms. What they remembered were the images Rima uses to teach such as "catch the bird's tail" or "fish in the water" (Fig. 73). I now ask for people to give pictures or images to dance in the T'ai Chi style. I suggest that they come from nature, but this is not necessary. From these pictures come impressionistic dances usually involving just arms. It can be done sitting or standing and can last a very long time.

POETRY: The images found in poetry can be evocative for dance improvisations. The group can share their favorite poems or write their own for the class to use. It is good to have the students already comfortable with improvisational techniques before introducing the richness of poetic imagery. Particularly useful are the skills associated with word dances and creating moods through dance.

Some older people have definite opinions about art. They might find this mixed media approach offensive. Once I tried to get a group to dance to a painting I brought. This particular group was usually responsive and quick to try new things. However, with this project they remained reticent. "I don't get what you mean; I can't dance to a picture," were the kind of comments offered. So, I did a dance to the painting and taught it to them. Later I learned that they simply were not interested in doing anything with pictures except look at them.

MUSIC: Music is a most basic place to get material. One just plays different styles and observes what happens. Any structure can be used.

PURE MOVEMENT: Like music, movement itself is material for improvisations. In other words, there does not have to be an idea each time an improvi-

Figure 73. Images from nature: the fish.

sation is done. To move with variations, as sculptures or as mirrors just for the dance itself is fine.

Designing successful improvisational structures is an art. It can be learned if one is willing to try new things and if one takes cues and ideas from the students. Anything is possible.

Chapter Seven

MORE CENTER WORK

AFTER the main improvisation segment, a class can proceed in several directions. Many factors contribute to the decision that the teacher makes at this point. He or she must gather a sense of the level of fatigue among those who have been dancing. Can they do more creative work? Can they dance longer on their feet? Do they need to rest, or can their stamina be stretched? For many older people, there are not many reasons to be active; therefore, it is good if the dance class can keep them on their feet and moving as a force against the sedentary existence of the rest of the week. They also gain confidence and self-approval if the stand-up part of class lasts a long time.

Balanced against this are the needs of the people who have been patiently watching the portion of class in which they do not participate. The people with walkers, wheelchairs, or a distaste for the improvisation are probably waiting for more work in the chairs or at least more structure. The decision may also depend on how much time is left. Performance takes at least fifteen minutes, while returning to the chairs may only take five.

Given these considerations, the teacher can choose from the following:

1. With fresh input from teacher and students, the improvisation can continue.
2. The class can divide up in small groups and present informal performances.
3. The teacher can teach a phrase or review a dance routine.
4. The group can do a dance based on folk forms, led by the teacher.
5. The group can return to the chairs and do something quieter in which everyone can participate.

Extending Improvisation

Sometimes an improvisation has not gone as well as the teacher anticipated it might. With direction from the teacher, comments from the students, a discussion of the problems, and potential for the structure, it is often useful to try it again.

At times the students get tired, but the improvisational idea or structure still remains exciting. In a situation such as this, it is possible to return to the chairs but continue improvising with slight changes in the structure to allow for students' energy levels.

Improvisation is such a flexible tool that almost any need a class has can be met by this form, providing students and teacher are thinking freshly in the moment.

Performance

Classroom performance provides a time for people to rehearse in small groups and show their work to the rest of the class. Besides being fun, performance gives the older people a sense that something is really happening, something slightly out of the ordinary. From the point of view of the art form, it is a useful way for the teacher to chart people's progress, both in actual movement ability and in the ways they approach different performance issues.

Most performance structures are, in fact, developments of the improvisations. Thus, building a phrase, sculptures, follow the leader, and words and movement combined are the base of many performances. What makes this different from improvisation is that there is an audience, the movements are somewhat repeatable, and some effort has been made to organize the material to communicate to someone else. Thus, aesthetic decision making is involved.

The performance process begins by dividing the class into smaller groups. These divisions can be arbitrary or based on the strengths of various students. It might be useful to place all the very active people in one group so that their work can be done standing with high energy, and perhaps all the people sitting would then form another group. It is occasionally good to mix the ability levels and see how the students combine their physical and expressive capabilities.

The group process of making a dance can seem mystifying at first, so it helps to keep the goals of the class clearly in mind. Just getting people up, preparing, and performing a short dance may be all that is necessary for success. After a while, however, people may want to hone their skills, and new kinds of artistic choices will come into play.

Very often as a group gathers to begin the planning, there will be silence. No one will want to take the first step and suggest a possible approach to the chosen theme. However, everyone's mind is probably full of ideas. If none will start, the teacher can assign someone to make the first comment, or the teacher can select a leader in each group for that evening. That person can see to it that the process moves along and might also take responsibility to give verbal cues during the performance so that people do not have to memorize the sequence of events.

With some reticent groups, it may be necessary for the teacher to take a very active role. In fact, at the Roosevelt, where I know the class members well, I will sometimes lead a smaller group of people who are generally nonresponsive. These students come to class regularly either to observe or to do a small portion of the exercises. Although people in this group do not actually develop the dance, I am able to generate some initiative in them. They perform by following, the rest of the class applauds, and in an important way they become participants in the class.

The descriptions of dances that follow are presented to give an idea of the range of responses and expectations for performance. As is evident from the four dances to be described, basic acceptance of people's ability is crucial to a good experience. The theme for these dances is the Fourth of July. Each group has approached the issue differently.

The first group starts in a sculpture with arms stretching out and up. Later they explain it is a firework. They move apart making a hissing sound, explode with a larger sound, and come back together again. The next movement has a longer, slower hissing quality that never explodes but returns together. In the third and last sequence they each separate and dance around, circling their hands as if they are holding sparklers. They hum or sing a patriotic song.

The second group stands in an amorphous configuration and yawns and stretches their arms as if waking up. Someone begins a stirring motion, and they all do it. It appears as if they are cooking and tasting, as some lick imaginary spoons and essentially mime the action. Someone starts walking away, while another remembers that the group planned to pack everything into a make-believe suitcase. The person walking giggles and returns to the packing. Then they all sort of wander around. Someone calls out, "Over here," and everyone begins to settle into preparations for a picnic. The dance ends as they eat.

The third group is the chair group. They are following an assistant's direction. They have built a phrase that is nine counts long, each movement expressing a Fourth of July remembrance. Many in the group cannot remember what comes next, but all follow along pretty well.

The fourth group stands in a circle. Each person steps into the middle and does a dance. One seems soft and airy, another strong and tense. When each has danced, they take hands in a circle and, with the help of the musician, dance a happy, quick series of steps, not in unison. Then they lift their arms into the air and bow. They announce that they each did a freedom dance, and they are glad to be independent.

One could ask how these groups arrived at their particular dances. Probably the starting point of each section was to ask what people think of when they think of the Fourth of July. These verbal responses are images that can then be turned into a dance. With practice, both teacher and students can begin to intuit which images work best in which structures.

The discussions that follow the performances can also be a helpful tool for learning what works best. For example, it is quite powerful to move in unison but not all the time. A group of dancers may decide that they want to end in unison or begin together and then separate into other structures. This they know from experience, both as performers and as audience.

These performances are not designed to be great art, though great moments happen. Each person is supported for his or her turn by an appreciative audience. What is seen here are some delightful dances and some very expressive moments. Sometimes ideas are found that if developed through rehearsal could become very good dances. That is not the goal of the class, however.

Fear of performing can be overcome in a supportive environment. It is interesting that the people who bring the most fear, feelings of competition, and need to be perfect are the younger dancers and assistants. This is unfortunate for two reasons. These attitudes affect the older dancers. They, too, become unnecessarily nervous and insecure. It is important to remember that these classroom performances are not formal dance concerts; they are based on improvisational dances and need to preserve the spontaneity of that form. They should not have the appearance of a well-rehearsed, cleaned dance phrase. If the group chooses to continue to practice the same dance in order to perform in a more public event, then it would be appropriate to seek ways of improving the appearance of the dance.

This undue fear on the part of the younger dancers reflects a rigidity in their approach to performing that is unfortunate for them and their dancing careers. It is important to distinguish the different kinds of performing situations and to use them to the best advantage. One of the wonderful things this work can offer a dancer is the freedom from some of the intensely difficult feelings that surround typical dance performances. To perform simply as a dancer, dancing without having to be best, perfect, better than anyone else, is very liberating. Competitive or fearful feelings may seem to be appropriate to performance in formal concert halls but not in the fluorescent-lighted room of a senior center.

Some teachers and students might be more comfortable when there is a thematic relationship between the first introduction, improvisation, and performance. For example, a class could use the Fourth of July theme, when people introduced themselves by giving a word and movement that was triggered by the thought of independence. They could then improvise on all of the words that came out of the introductions. Finally, in small groups they could prepare performances. This connection is not necessary for every class. In fact, it is important not to be rigid in approach.

Teaching a Phrase or Reviewing a Dance Routine

Teaching a phrase or reviewing a routine can be very satisfying for both students and teacher. The teacher can teach a phrase and practice it over and over with the students for several weeks. This challenges people's memories, as well as their abilities to master movement over a longer period of time. It is important, however, that students succeed on some level immediately, so one should create the movement experience with that in mind.

Figure 74. *Swan Lake.*
PHOTO: DeLoria

One of the favorite dances at the Roosevelt is a variation on the "four swans" from *Swan Lake* (Fig. 74). The teacher should teach the movements in a circle, with participants holding hands at first. It consists of four sections:

1. Practice passés, four times on each leg. (Passé is bringing the toe of one leg to the side of the knee of the standing leg. See stand-up warm-ups for review.)
2. Turn head to right, up to ceiling, to the left, and back to center. Reverse.
3. Try combining head movements and passés. (This is very difficult, and people will only succeed after a long time. This step is optional.)
4. Passé and touch the toe to the floor in front.
   Passé and touch the toe to the floor to the side.
   Passé and touch the toe to the floor in back.
   Passé and return the foot to the center standing position.

Then the class forms groups of three, four, or five people and holds hands in ice skater fashion. This is done by standing close to each other and opening the arms wide. Each person holds the hand of the person two people away from him or her. The people on the end bring their outside hand to the person next to them. The class should practice the dance in this formation and practice an elaborate bow.

Many dances can be adapted. New ones can be choreographed for older people. Also, if the teacher remembers from week to week, phrases can be built by the students and rehearsed as dances put to special music. Some students will remember a phrase, but it is helpful if the teacher also learns it. Together they can take responsibility for remembering and teaching it the next week.

Dances Based on Folk Forms

An alternative to performance or routine is a simply structured group dance based on folk forms (Fig. 75). Adapting traditional forms can be fun, lively, and simple enough for everyone to do. In fact, the simpler, the better. Often these dances consist of people holding hands in circles or lines and walking. The teacher becomes a kind of square-dance caller. Couples can make arches for others to pass under. Lines can travel around the room or even down the hall and back.

If the group is in a circle, a popular structure is to get everyone into the center and back again. There is great contact in this form, and simple variations can be suggested on each walk to the center. This structure can also work if everyone is in two lines, as in the Virginia Reel. Again, variations can be called as partners come towards each other and then back away.

If assistants are available, some of the less physically stable people can join this dance. In this case, the assistant and the person needing help together form one-half of a couple. In effect, they dance as one person.

Returning to the Chairs

Returning to the chairs is the signal that the end of class is approaching. It is always good to do one last dance together. This could be a repetition of the phrase the class built earlier or a completely new movement idea. The length of this dance depends on people's attention spans and energy levels.

Before closing the class, it is sometimes good to solicit comments from the students about how they are feeling, what they thought about class, or what successes or problems they might be having with dance. It is appropriate for the teacher also to speak of these things. General improvement in the students' ability is a good thing to mention publicly. Some of this conversation will be repeated privately after class, if the teacher makes himself or herself available to the students. Other students would prefer raising their questions in private anyway and will wait until after class to talk or arrange to meet the teacher be-

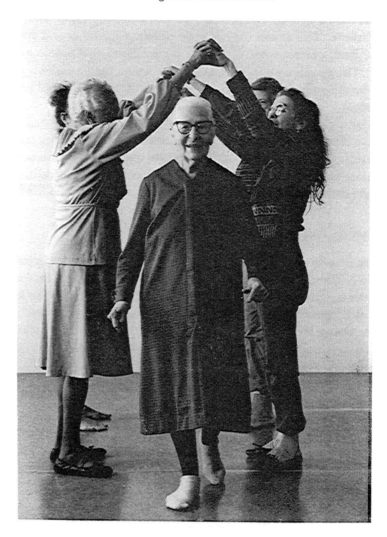

Figure 75. Dance based on folk forms.
PHOTO: DeLoria

fore class the next week. The teacher should close the class with "Thank you, see you next week" or similar statement.

Some older people might be reluctant to let the teacher leave. They will engage the dancer in a long discussion about their physical pain or some event that an improvisation theme may have triggered. Initially, the conversation may be about class, but it is very easy for some older people to wander and simply talk because someone is listening. The teacher will need to decide how to resolve these incidents. It is OK to listen sometimes, and it is also all right to pull one's hand away and say simply, "I have to go now, see you next week." The dancer is there to teach dance, not solve the intense personal problems of some individuals in the class.

Chapter Eight

PUBLIC DEMONSTRATION AND PERFORMANCE: THE DANCERS OF THE THIRD AGE

THE first response to the dance classes at the Roosevelt came from other organizations serving senior adults who sought ideas for their own programs. Interested dancers, actors, visual artists, and poets also came, wanting ideas for similar projects. In response to the questions and requests for dance programs, a demonstration group from the Roosevelt class was formed.

The initial demonstrations took place at senior citizen centers. They consisted of a typical class, led by the dance teacher and assisted by members of the Roosevelt group. The size of this troupe varied from four to fifteen. Any member of the Roosevelt class who was free on a demonstration day was welcome to come.

These demonstrations were geared completely towards participation by the audience. Occasionally, the Roosevelt people danced alone in order to show an improvisation, but the idea was to get the audience convinced that they, too, could dance. The Roosevelt group itself was less than a year old at that time. Therefore, the demonstrations were simple, the exercises and the improvisations lasting a very short time.

The audiences and sponsoring organizations were happy with the results of these demonstrations. The performing group was not. They began to critique the experience and asked for rehearsal time in order to improve the "show." This was the beginning of the performance company eventually called the Dancers of the Third Age.

The difference between demonstration and performance is mainly a matter of intent and time. A demonstration group needs no rehearsal, although the leader must be well prepared. The group does need to know what the leader means when he or she asks for certain things, but basically it is a public class

123

held for a group of interested people. A performance group might do the same things as a demonstration group, but they are rehearsed, prepared to do improvisations and perhaps some extra dances learned and practiced.

The effects of a performance group growing out of ongoing classes can be significant. Students become more committed. There is a dramatic change in people's willingness to participate, openness to new directions and instruction, and recognition of the importance of the work. Performing can be a goal for a dance teacher for his or her students in a senior adult class, but it is not absolutely necessary.

The following description of a typical Dancers of the Third Age performance briefly explains format, motivation, and structure. The discussion will be brief, since the intent of this book is to describe dance classes. It is offered here as a logical development to any modern dance class for seniors.

There are two goals to the performance of the Dancers of the Third Age. First is to show people that senior adults are vital, active citizens. The second is to introduce the audiences to the world of modern dance. The combination of these two elements is usually an inspiring and joyful event. The senior dancers convince people that dance is indeed for everyone and that its expressive power is significant. Joined by the strong and capable dancing of the professional Dance Exchange Performance Company members, the performances can be touching and affirming of human potential.

Over the years there have been some twenty-five senior adults active in performance. Of these, one has died, nine have moved away, and five have dropped out for health reasons. New people are brought into the troupe as they become ready in their regular dance classes or by expressing an interest in the program and getting in touch with the sponsoring organization, the Dance Exchange. From four to eight senior adults perform in each show.

Time is set aside during the year to find new material for the show. Story sessions are held, and each dancer comes with ideas for possible dances. Often these ideas are openly rehearsed in performance as works in progress.

A typical performance begins with introductions. The leader starts with a talking dance and, depending on the audience, gives different background information. This usually includes a description of the Dance Exchange and mention of the ninety-five-year age range of its students. The leader will say, or his or her dancing will make clear, that moving with so many different kinds of people is exciting. Then each member of the troupe introduces himself or herself. Again, these are danced and spoken simultaneously. For example, Vee giggles, wiggles, and says she is the rascal of the group. Ada describes being in Japan during the war and shows how the women walked and greeted each other. John recites a poem and then dances the last line. Thelma usually gives her age, which often brings gasps from the audience. One of the younger performers announces while moving quickly through the space that he is ninety years old and living proof that dancing keeps one young. Others in the group vary their stories. It is always interesting to see what people will do.

The introductions are followed by a warm-up that involves performers and audience. The length and content of this varies according to the audience. For young children it is kept brief and done with variations in tempo to keep their interest. Older children are told anecdotes about getting older and the way bodies begin to respond to dance after years of inactivity. The warm-up part of the show is lengthened for senior adult audiences. The structure of the exercises is an easier way for them to participate than the improvisations that follow. They are given frequent rests.

Older dancers are asked to lead certain sections of the warm-up. John has a very funny adaptation of karate movements. He does it slowly with one finger indicating the shape of the movement in a half-hearted fashion. This provides an opportunity to discuss the uniqueness of each person's style and theme and variation as a choreographic tool. It also pokes fun at exercise fanatics.

After warm-up, the audience and performers build a phrase together. If people from the audience do not suggest a movement, one is selected by the leader, who observes a movement gesture by a member of the audience and uses the gesture as a count of the phrase. The dance is then performed slowly and quickly. The difficulty of the fast movements delights the audience and provides an example of how hard dance really is.

The middle section of the performance includes dance stories, improvisations, and audience participation dances. The order of the show depends on the audience. Quiet moments are interspersed with dances that bring excitement and energy to the viewer. Among the stories is a simple tale of chopping wood in Northern Michigan, where Harry grew up. At the end of Harry's elaborate description of how to cut down a dead tree, he calls, "Timber," and several people fall to the floor. Rehearsing this story confirmed the idea that people will work to stretch their ability if they are motivated to do so. Since the dance requires people to fall to the floor, the seniors had to learn how to get up and down comfortably. This was very difficult for many in the group. In fact, in performance only two will do it, but in rehearsal, everyone tried it. One said after the first time he got up from the floor, "Pretty soon I'll be able to take a bath again."

Olena's story is about her great uncle, a mailman in Russia at the turn of the century. He must take the mail through the forest, where he is accosted by a bear. Betty and Jess have each played the bear, a creature more interested in licking the mailman than eating him. It is a favorite story with children, since all members of the troupe dance different animals and other living things of the forest. It is quite wonderful to see Ada's cat (Fig. 76), Lee's hawk, Thelma's forest, John's giant mushroom, and Vee's squirrel. This story also displays the importance of the younger dancers to the group's success. Although the part is

Figure 76 . Ada's cat from *The Bear Story*.

simple, the absolute conviction that Don carries as the mailman is the pivotal point of the dance. His fear of the bear and his own humorous resolution of the dance make the whole piece work.

In addition to the improvisational skills required of the young performers, several dances demand technical skills, too. The dance requiring the most technical skill for a younger performer is *Who's on First*, a dance about sports and art. In it, Don's stylized dancing is backed by the company's expressive view of sports fans. The quality the older people bring to this outrageous behavior is what makes the dance succeed.

The improvisational nature of the show allows everyone to remain natural. This is very important for people who are not trained performers. As long as they feel comfortable and know that even "mistakes" are OK, the nervousness that can ruin a performance is eliminated.

The same improvisational structures are done in each performance, such as word dances, sculptures, or mirrors. The dances change with each show based on people's mood, audience response, and the motivation of the improvisation. Sculptures are done first. Here, after the company has set up the first sculpture, participation is requested from the audience. Children are eager to join, older people less so. Usually one or two people will try it to the delight of their peers. A high point of the performance is asking for teachers to participate. When the children understand that we are requesting the adults to join in, a wild scene ensues in which different groups of children yell for favorite teachers to become involved. As exciting as the selection process is, when the teachers actually begin to dance, there is so much laughter and applause that it is sometimes difficult to hear the music. It is a marvelously democratic moment, as dance becomes the equalizer, and teacher and student, old and young, trained and untrained, move together in a series of dances and freezes that connect all to one another. The older people establish such a sense of safety, and a feeling of "if they can do it, so can I," that the participation becomes easy and natural.

The performance shows that dance is fun, requires skill, can involve many people, and can tell a story. It also shows that it is a way for people to share feelings that might be difficult to do in another way. This is particularly true of the dance called *Transformations* (Figs. 77 through 81). In this, the older people

Figure 77. Beginning of *Transformations*.

Figure 78. *Transformations.*

present the clichés and stereotypes that make up the reality of the lives of some American older adults. They become characters that appear to be disoriented, depressed, and unable to move. During the dance they begin to hear the music and slowly transform to the kind of human beings they each see themselves to be. At the end they all hold hands and dance together.

The performance ends with two dances. One, taught by Thelma, is a dance she learned in 1913. Called *Ballin' the Jack*, it is a popular dance done with a song (Fig. 82). The words of the song tell the dancer what to do: "Put your knees together, close up tight. Swing them to the left and swing them to the right," etc. The lineup of performers dancing "show biz" style is fun. In some performances a variation is done with this dance so that the words "put your knees together" are danced in a completely different way. Rock 'n' roll and expressive modern dance style are two of the variations possible. Later, the entire audience is taught the dance.

The last dance, *The Rainbow*, consists of a simple routine using images of rainbows and stars (Fig. 83). Then each dancer takes a part of the pot of gold and dances with it. At the conclusion of the dance, the gold is given either to an

Figure 79. *Transformations.*

audience member or to the musician. Here, each dancer's unique style and approach to movement is explored.

The Dancers of the Third Age performance lasts anywhere from thirty
minutes to an hour. Other more formal dances may be included. There are occasions when just the younger people dance. There are periods when the audience can ask questions. It, like the entire senior program, is very flexible.

Figure 80. *Transformations.*

Figure 81. *Transformations.*

Figure 82. "Swing them to the right . . . " from *Ballin' the Jack*.
PHOTO: DeLoria

Figure 83. The *Rainbow*.
PHOTO: Reinhardt

AUDIENCE RESPONSE

The Dancers of the Third Age have danced for children and senior adults. They have performed for sympathetic organizations such as the National Council on the Aging, Foster Grandparents, Gray Panthers, and the National Committee for Arts and the Handicapped. They have performed alongside preprofessional college dance majors, recognized modern dance troupes, and national theater groups. The reception is almost always positive. The children write letters often accompanied with drawings of their favorite dance or performer.

Figure 84. Rehearsal at the Dance Exchange.
PHOTO: DeLoria

The middle grade children indicate an interest in becoming involved with such a group. One young girl wrote, "Well, I think the program was very enjoyable, funny and I wish I could see it again with my grandparents. When I grow up maybe I would like to have a dance studio for elders. . . . " Another commented, "I enjoyed your dancing, and I hope you come again. When I am a senior citizen, I want to dance like you." The funniest comment came from a young boy who said, "Some parts were funny. Some things you did were remarkable. p.s. I'm not 86, so I can't do those pushups. . . ."

The teachers also like the program. From a sixth-grade teacher, I received the following: "I for one feel that all of our lives were enriched by the experience. It takes 'guts' to be 70 or 80 and deviate from lifelong established patterns, in some instances, and become involved in something new. Contrary to the adage, one can teach an old dog new tricks. I certainly do hope they come again."

After the troupe performed at the National Conference of the National Committee for the Arts and the Handicapped, the following comment was made by its executive director, Bette Valenti:

> Bravo. Your performance at our NCAH Annual Meeting was a smashing success and helped us all revise our restricted stereotypes of older persons.
> We believe that older Americans can contribute greatly to efforts to reach handicapped children and youth through the arts. This intergenerational joining of hands holds great promise. Your experiences illustrate the power of the arts to touch us all.

The Dancers of the Third Age have generated enough interest that on several occasions journalists have come to a few performances and then written articles about the company. The following is excerpted from the George Washington University newspaper, *The Hatchet* (Faske, 1978).

> The most beautiful and inspiring dance group around is one that few have seen, or rather experienced. Out of the ordinary, yes, but not because its style is avant garde, or improvisational or gimmicky. The eight performers that comprise the group are each over 60 years old . . . and they are beautiful.

As wonderful as intergenerational performance is for the audience, the feeling of value that this experience brings to the members of the troupe, old and young, is at the heart of its success. That is what makes it worth the struggle to arrange transportation and performance dates, get the special needs of the group meet by the sponsors, remind the performers of their commitment, and give up the very valuable time to the weekly shows.

FORMAL CONCERTS

The senior adult dancers of the Dancers of the Third Age sometimes join the Dance Exchange Performance Company in formal concerts. This professional company performs in formal spaces such as the Kennedy Center's Terrace Theater and in less formal spaces such as lofts, community halls, and schools (Fig. 85).

The format of the material is more structured and complex than the Dancers of the Third Age show. It is best seen with formal lighting and costumes. The dances themselves are technically more demanding and require a different concentration from both performer and audience. The audience takes on a more conventional role by paying admission and by being observers of the concert, rather than participants.

Despite the heavy rehearsal schedule and pressure that surrounds the struc-

Figure 85. Rehearsal at the O'Neill Theater Center Choreographers' Conference; Thelma Tulane, Paul Sarvis, Liz Lerman.

PHOTO: Migdoll

tured events of the Dance Exchange Performance Company, almost every dance in the company repertory involves older people in some way. Their parts might be small, such as those of visitors in a dance about art galleries, but in other pieces the older performers dance major roles.

This means that the seniors are subjected to the same high and low points as any performing artist. Positive and negative reactions from friends and critics, excitement, and exhaustion become a part of their lives.

The Dance Exchange Performance Company is frequently reviewed by the dance critics, so there has been a process of writing about the presence of the elderly on the stage.

Two reviews are excerpted here as examples of how critics can view older dancers in formal productions. The first, written by Ginna Browne in the *Columbia Flier* is about *Ms. Galaxy and her Three Raps with God* and appeared in 1977. The second is written by Alan Kriegsman and appears in *The Washington Post* in 1978 and concerns the dance *Elevator Operator and Other Strangers* (Fig. 86).

> Among the most delightful performers were the group of senior citizens from the Roosevelt Hotel who have been studying dance with Lerman for nearly two years. They danced with the younger members of the company who showed warm respect and awareness for their contributions to the production. At times these elderly terpsichoreans stole the show.[1]

> The elevator operator, so engagingly portrayed by Harry Belanger, one of the senior citizens Lerman likes to recruit into performance, is the emblem of the passing world.[2]

Not all of the reviews about the Dance Exchange Performance Company are positive, but the comments about the older people usually are. However,

Figure 86. Harry Belanger, Helen Rea, Colette Yglesias in *Elevator Operator and Other Strangers*.
Photo: DeLoria

---

[1]From Ginna Browne, "*Ms. Galaxy and Her Three Raps with God*", the *Columbia Flier*, June 23, 1977, p. 30.
[2]From Alan Kriegsman, "Liz Lerman", the *Washington Post*, April 14, 1978, p. B6.

one dance writer from the metropolitan area of Washington, D.C., in conversation was totally against the incorporation of the older dancers into concert works. She said that in the dance *Ms. Galaxy and Her Three Raps with God* one of the women had entered the stage wearing a shawl just like the kind her grandmother used to wear. The memory of her grandmother had made her cry during the entire dance. As a consequence, she did not think that the dance was a work of art.

The performance, whether formal or informal, is the goal that brings together all the other work (Fig. 87). The technique classes make sense. The rehearsal and the consequent discipine make sense. The conversation during the car rides to and from performances enrich the lives of this intergenerational group, and dancing together before an audience is a wonderful experience.

Figure 87. *Bonsai* with Vee Hallenbeck and Thelma Tulane.
PHOTO: DeLoria

Chapter Nine

BENEFITS FOR OLDER
AND YOUNGER DANCERS

I used to be shy and timid. Then I started to dance with the Dance Exchange, and all of a sudden I was blossoming," says a woman in her eighties. She began dance class with one arm in a sling. After it healed, she became part of the performing troupe and continues to attend dance class regularly. She has learned to budget her strength and does not tour with each performance. She does use every opportunity to see the world and comment about it. Of all the older people dancing, this woman has developed the most ideas about choreography. She conceptualizes dances frequently, saying, "Wouldn't it be fun if we could make a dance about — — — ." Her imagination is constantly functioning.

Just the other day, we were in the car on the way to a photo session. She started exclaiming about the beautiful white house with the rickety fence. I did not see one, as we were driving past the embassies on 16th Street. Then she pointed skyward, and it was apparent she was gazing at the clouds. She laughed and said, "I think some people would say I'm crazy the way I look at things; everyone except you. You encourage it, and I have so much fun because I see the dance in everything." ·

Everyone has reasons to dance. The benefits from the dance classes for the elderly do not go unnoticed by the senior adults. They say it improves their social outlook, physical well-being, and sense of personal worth. For some it has opened a new field of endeavor, and so they see themselves developing an artistic sense and a knowledge of the dance.

The younger dancers have also been quick to describe the benefits they experience from working with the older people. They reflect on how it has affected their dancing, performing, teaching, and choreography. There is also a feeling that this work affects them on a social level, giving them a different sense of self-worth.

In this chapter the participants speak. The first half is devoted to the reasons the senior adults continue to dance. The second half describes the work of the younger dancers and their gains from their association with the elderly.

VIEWS OF THE OLDER DANCER

Social Reasons for Dancing

"Oh, there's certainly no generation gap here. This group of youngsters and oldsters feel just at home and we enjoy each other very much." This comment, by eighty-four-year-old Harry, is simple and true. For Harry, the involvement with people unlike himself is an important part of the dance activity, but it is more profound than simply the joy he and others feel. Harry has also said, "At the end of the sixties I used to think the young people of this country were going to the dogs, but I've changed my mind, because of my association with the Dance Exchange." With dance as the common ground, and with performance and the routine of classes the common goal, people who would normally have little or no reason to talk to each other instead have a very rich life together.

Harry's reflections on the generation gap and the way dance is a bridge across this gap suggest some of the real power inherent in this experience. The dancing allows the formation of a little community. It is a group of people who come together for certain reasons, to meet certain goals, guided by a shared institution, with each member feeling that they have some choice in the outcome. This is an important issue in anyone's life, especially older people who have been stripped of much of the autonomy and power by our society.

For other seniors, there are intense personal reasons for enjoying the dance. Thelma, who joined the dance class at age eighty, came to the Roosevelt after the death of her husband. "I was kind of, you know, depressed. Coming in contact with dance has changed my life completely. It gave me a new outlook on life, and I enjoy the exercises." At first, Thelma came only to the evening class. Later, though, after a general invitation to all students to come to an open rehearsal, Thema describes; "And, as I say, curiosity killed a cat. So I went on up to see what was going on, and before I left I belonged to the group. And I started, you know, with the exercises and traveling around to the different schools and auditoriums and places like that with the group. And I really like it. It just gave me a new life."

For Sue, a woman with a disability who rarely goes out anymore, the dance class is a time when "interesting" people gather. It's not just the "same old conversations."

John, a former naval commander, considers the dance class a time of social relaxation and fun, something that "comes regularly." He particularly likes meeting the younger dancers. John stays in touch with many younger people who leave the program. He asks frequently for people of whom he is especially fond. John is the official welcomer. He sits next to any visitor to the class and gives them historical background.

Some people come to dance class for individual reasons. One night after the author had been at the Roosevelt for about half a year, an older man approached her after class and asked for help with his golf swing. She showed him some loosening up exercises he could do every day before he went out on the course. Actually, this man probably did not still golf, but the dancing and simulation of the golf movement, which he continued to do alone in his room approximated some of the exhilaration he used to feel.

Physical Reasons for Dancing

> Dancing has brought me back to life. . . . Dance class has brought me many new friends, but that's not all. I had severe arthritis and for years I couldn't walk up stairs, and my arms were so crippled that I couldn't put my hands behind my back. At first I didn't do much dancing, but little by little I found I could move more and more. Then suddenly one day I found I could put my hand behind my back and I was absolutely amazed.[1]

So Vee describes her dance experience. Vee could not walk up stairs when she began dancing. Now she is a member of the touring company, having traveled as far as Boston, Massachusetts, and St. Petersburg, Florida. There are other stories, including a wheelchair-bound person who has grown strong and confident enough to dance part of class standing up.

Originally, the class consisted of ten minutes of dance instruction and then a few minutes of performance by the teacher. This tradeoff helped keep people interested and allowed resting time. As classes continued, more and more of the students just joined the teacher's miniperformance until it became clear that class could last forty-five minutes to an hour without major pauses.

Different students work on different issues. For one student, arthritis is the foe that has to be overcome. She uses the T'ai Chi period as a time to work on continuous movement of both arms, trying to keep one more active than the other. Another works to get certain feet combinations, especially *Swan Lake*.

One participant made extraordinary strides in her ability to move, as well as speak. Disabled by both severe scoliosis and a stroke, this woman talked haltingly and moved in basically the same pattern every week. Over a six-month period, each time she was given the opportunity to introduce herself, she was able to tell more and more of her story as well as increase the kind of move-

---

[1]From Carol Krucoff, "Senior Citizens Say Dancing Puts Them 'On Top of the World,'" the *Washington Post*, May 26, 1977, p. DC4.

ments she did. She was particularly impressive in performance, where she used the attention of the audience to her best advantage. I would wait with curiosity for each of her introductions because I learned more about her with each show.

Her balance, however, never improved. After several falls while on tour, she had to be asked to stop performing, since she would require a full-time companion to be able to continue. Thus, although the dancing took her far, it did not or could not solve all the physical problems confronting her.

Humanitarian Reasons for Dancing

For some of the older people, especially those performing, there is a desire to continue because they feel useful. To them, dancing is something to share with others. As one participant said: "I think all of us have a feeling we're glad to be here, and we want to do this, and I think that's contagious. Now in Baltimore, for instance, there are older people there, and we did a certain performance . . . we said, 'Come on, dance.' And they came out and danced with us . . . so the thing is, I think they really enjoy it as a whole." This is Ada's description of a trip to the Waxter Center in Baltimore. For some of the seniors, it is dancing for older people that is most rewarding. For others, it is the children they most enjoy. John once said that he loved their "unrestrained appreciation" and was happy to show the little ones what the "old ones" can really do.

Mary has been in a wheelchair since I met her, and she travelled with the group until she moved away. Her feelings about performing and its importance to her reflect her attitude that education is a large part of what the dancing is about:

> I usually say that no matter what shape you're in, there is always something that you can do, and that helps get across to the kids to participate, to be active. Don't sit back and let the world go by.
> I think there is a natural hesitation and rejection of handicapped people. They [the kids] have to get over that. . . . It's their problem about how to respond, but since I recognize it I try to minimize it. In that short time [length of one performance] they may be aware that a person with a handicap can perform and be active. But it's hard to overcome a lifetime of looking the other way.

Harry and Thelma were asked to travel to upstate New York to give a workshop for older people. Thelma says,

> We just showed them how they could breathe. We showed them that they could start the slow motion, how they could exercise their shoulders, their arms, their hips, their legs and their feet. And then we showed them one or two of the parts in the dances that we do, to show that they could take part.

Harry adds with pride,

> That day we put on three different shows. One for the college. Then we went to a senior citizen's home and did it there. And in the afternoon we went to a nursing home.

Artistic Reasons for Dancing

For those who have joined the Dancers of the Third Age, the motivation for dancing focuses around the performances. They each like different parts of the show or the process involved in choreographing for it. Mary liked the improvisations the best. She thought about them outside of rehearsals and performance and often came to me with suggestions for improvement. Before she moved away she said, "I just love the improvisation. It's an opportunity to do something, express ourselves and also to think of ways in which the audience might participate. It's an opportunity to do something that isn't written down and set for us to do."

Thelma describes how dancing "becomes a part of me. I can just go on with it and not worry about whether I am doing it right or wrong. It just feels like myself."

Harry, on the other hand, worried a lot about his work. He wrote everything down and practiced by himself. "Well, it was harder for me to get used to slow movements, which happen sometimes in modern dance. Whereas mine were almost always quick, sharp, you know. In the dance the way it is nowadays we occasionally have to do slow movements."

In general, all of the dancers think more about professional dance and watch it on TV whenever possible. Mary once said, "I watch dance on television. . . . Unless you have seen the steps worked on and know how long it takes to achieve this profession, you would not be aware of the marvelous quality they have." When transportation is available, most like to go out and see dance now, with a different kind of appreciation than before.

What all of these comments indicate is an interest in something and the pride they have in mastering it, a commendable activity for any age group.

VIEWS OF THE YOUNGER DANCER

For younger dancers there are many reasons to work with the older adult and many benefits. It affects their dancing, their performing, their teaching, their attitudes about dance, and the value they place on the meaning of their lives. Without these benefits, the dance class program for senior adults would not work.

Dancing with Older Dancers

The most often heard comment from a younger dancer who comes to the Roosevelt is, "I've never been so loose. I've never been able to feel so light when

I jump, or get my leg so high. I feel so good while I'm dancing." This is a most important issue for the younger dancer. The senior adult audience is supportive, affirming, and able to give very strong, loving attention. The result is a kind of refuge from critics, which allows the dancer an emotional release and freedom of movement. This is not to suggest that older people cannot be critical, because they can be and are, nor does it mean that there are not times when criticism is important for the training dancer. However, there are also times when complete approval is appropriate for the young training artist, and often the senior citizen center is a place where this can take place. There is a lesson to be learned for the dancer who can transfer the strength of this movement to other more charged and competitive environments.

The older people also teach younger dancers about expression. Don Zuckerman said: "I became aware that there is more to dancing than how you use your body. Watching them [older dancers] be so effective without a lot of technical power left me room to try it too. The whole person can affect a dance too, not just the physical body."

Performance with Older Dancers

Working with the senior adult as co-performer requires of the young dancer a dual focus. The usual internal focus, or concentration, that comes from any dance task is necessary if the dancer is to perform. The second, an external peripheral focus, is necessary to maintain a connection with the older dancers. This connection goes beyond the typical requirement of any ensemble work. The older dancers often depend on the younger people for cues. The younger dancer must be constantly aware of safety precautions, especially issues of balance and stamina.

Meanwhile, the younger dancer has his or her own part to sustain. This is true in either improvisation or structured performance. It is not an easy thing to learn. Helen Rea comments, "You have to stay more aware of them than of yourself. That's important. You can't stay in your own little world."

The development of this dual focus is very important for a dancer. Many performing situations demand this capability. In certain dramatic roles one must carry on an internal/external focus to stay connected with the dance, other performers, and the audience. In some performing halls it is necessary to be able to relate directly to an audience. This is particularly true in most modern dance performing spaces, which are quite intimate.

This ability to keep an external focus and an internal concentration is not effectively taught in modern dance technique classes. The work with older adults will help a dancer learn this skill, since it is inherent in every aspect of the training.

Teaching Older Dancers

"Teaching older people has encouraged me to isolate the important ideas in my lessons. Only then can I adapt them. In that process I find out a lot about the material I use." Don's comment points out how the older person forces a younger dancer to consider what for years has been rote exercise or unquestioned assumptions. There are simply certain things dancers do in class. Suddenly, however, one must ask why, and this questioning can be very important for the dancer's personal use as well. "I'm learning what's limiting to them, finding the essential of dance. More aware of the real basic quality of dance," said Bob Fogelgren.

Teaching older people can be very demanding. It means changing habit patterns of one's teaching and dancing. Many older people are hearing impaired. In order to reach them, one must speak forcefully and in a low register, since high-pitched tones are lost. In order to keep people's attention in a crowded room where much activity is going on, it is sometimes necessary to appear larger than life and to exhibit a high level of energy. The ability to turn on this energy or to speak strongly, on call, is very useful.

When a person is able to change a habit or break a routine, it can lead to changes in other aspects of life. The older people make a safe environment in which younger people can grow. A quiet, soft-moving dancer can become less afraid to make a strong, powerful physical statement; a fast-paced dancer can learn to slow down and be patient.

All teaching experiences require that a person be able to make split-second decisions. While watching a movement, dance teachers are usually considering what to do next. In a class filled with as many different body types and needs as a group of senior adults, this moment is intensified. Sometimes a teacher might try, and discard, several different approaches or ideas for movement within the space of a minute.

Knowing what to say to an older person, when to say it, and how often to say it depends on the intuitive and developing sensitivity of the young dancer. Balancing their own ability to inspire and at the same time foster independence in the student are constant issues in these classes. It is very challenging and worthwhile to achieve. Bob Fogelgren, an instructor, says, "They are exciting and comfortable to teach. They're eager to learn. I'm teaching, but they're always willing to comment about class at any time and in unexpected ways."

Choreography with Older Dancers

Working with less technical dancers can be challenging for choreographers. Older people can bring expression, images, daring, and risk to a dance. They can also force the choreographer to develop scripts for performance that allow them to be natural and yet stageworthy. This is a very creative challenge.

Figure 88. Rehearsal of *Woman of the Clear Vision*.
Photo: DeLoria

If the seniors themselves do not appeal to the choreographer as potential dancers, their stories and ways of moving might. There is much in the way of creative material present in a class for seniors. Characterizations, movement idioms, expressive habits, and relationships can serve a choreographer.

I find the trips to the Roosevelt and other senior centers to be intense. The feeling aroused and the state I find myself in can sometimes initiate incredible movement sequences. To put oneself in the world and respond is an important thing for a creative artist to do. The combination of emotional safety I feel around old people and the images I see surrounding their lives provides an incredible landscape for choreographic work. This creative tension is valuable to me as a choreographer.

Social Reasons for Working with Older Dancers

Just as it is important for the older people to be with the young, the young dancers speak frequently of their joy in being with the seniors. "It makes a difference to me to be with people my grandparents' age. They have a lot to teach me, and their stories are amazing." This comment, from a younger dancer who worked in the program at its beginning stage, is typical. It becomes even more apparent in the performances in the schools where three or four generations are dancing together at one time. Then the sense of community is great. For some, it is the only time when this intergenerational experience exists.

There is much to learn from the older people. Stories of escaping from Germany, being a WAC in Japan during the occupation, living in the Great Depression, getting an education as a woman in the early part of the century are told between performances or before class.

On another level, watching the older people cope with the information brought to them by the dancers is also interesting. Don said, "You can come to appreciate small changes in attitudes. Watching them make new discoveries, even at their age, is very inspiring." At times the younger people feel as if they are the only contact with the outside world, other than TV. The older people soak up any comments about city politics, dance world happenings, or family tidbits that younger dancers are willing to share.

Earning a Livelihood while Working with Older Dancers

Dancers are poor. There is very little money available to pay people to dance. A bit more money is available to pay dancers to teach. In the past this has meant teaching those who can afford to learn or those who can afford to send their children to learn. Dancers are skilled. It takes years to make a dancer. It takes a lifetime to maintain those skills. No other profession is as demanding and pays so little to those who perservere. As long as dancers, and the communities they live in, continue to view the "real" dance as that which involves itself purely with performance, and performance training, the economic situation of the dancer will not change, nor will the richness of the dancer's life reach beyond the small enclaves that now experience this art form.

The Dance Exchange work with senior adults is a good model for a different approach to these issues. Committed dance performers are teaching a population that wants to be part of their world. Eager to learn, the older people give more than most students. Although as a group they do not have much money to support the teaching, the organizations that serve them are aware of the benefits of the dancing and are beginning to care enough to raise money to establish the classes.

The Value of Working with Older Dancers

People want meaning in their lives. For many training dancers, one of the things that plagues them is the amount of time required working on oneself and one's body. This can generate a sense of guilt, which is compounded by the necessity of maintaining that skill through years of technique classes.

The work with the older people can provide a balance to this. It does not require a full-time commitment, although it does ask for a regular commitment. For some dancers, this giving of information and watching the subsequent changes in the older people is just the right antidote to the feeling of isolation they have about themselves as dancers.

In relation to this, dancers can feel a very direct connection between their dancing and the joy it can bring to an audience. Once, after a class improvisation, an older person turned to one of the young visitors and told her she was a vision of grace. The young woman later told me that she did not realize her dancing could affect people so much. It made her feel wonderful.

As Robert Nisbet (1953) has pointed out in his book *The Quest for Community* it is only since the beginning of the modern European world that the popular myth has risen that places the artist in an isolated, solitary existence. Nisbet suggests that this development is a romantic ideal. Somehow, it became important to our society to claim that "artistic achievement is always connected in some degree with rootlessness and alienation, that art itself is asocial." He claims that this belief has disguised the actual "context of creative imagination" (p. 236).

The Dance Exchange program demonstrates that the senior center is a context for many creative imaginations. It offers a place for learning to dance better, a place where teachers can learn to teach, a place where dancers can bring the gift of their art to a receptive audience, a place where people's stories and life experiences offer a host of ideas for dances, a place where unique ways of dancing can be seen by any interested eye and used to develop dances that can be taken to a wider audience. It is then possible to educate that audience to an appreciation for the senior adult as a creative individual who can use the art form of dance as a medium of expression.

Chapter Ten

REFLECTIONS ON THE FUTURE

IN the eight years I have been teaching dance to seniors, there have been moments when theory and reality have joined. At those times I have felt that the effort is worth it, that the goal is clear, that the idea is right, and above all that it is possible. Some moments in the performances of older dancers are magic. When Harry entered his elevator at the beginning of each performance of *Elevator Operators and Other Strangers* and began his ritual "good morning," while exactly replicating the movements of his character, my body tensed with the excitement of a truly wonderful performance. When Helen and Thelma dance their duet in *Bonsai*, I know that the dance between generations and the passing on of knowledge continues forever through the faces and bodies of these two women. When Sol gets up in dance class to lead a phrase and learns as he does the power of leadership and of his own capability, I am satisfied. When I watch Jess, Vee, Thelma, and Judy dance the spirits welcoming my mother beyond her death, I know that there are dances that only old people can do and no amount of technique can bring a gifted young dancer to that place. Only time can do that.

This dance program is significant for both the elderly and arts communities. The number of older people in America is increasing at a rapid rate. New programs are needed, especially ones that can produce results and are cost effective. Dancers and their colleagues in other arts fields are in constant economic insecurity. The eighties are a decade that will witness a decreased role of government funding for the arts. Dancers must find ways to make people care about their survival so that they will contribute financial support. For the artist, this means fund raising, grant seeking, or producing revenues in a way compatible to their art form, still leaving time for their creative work.

This program for senior adults serves as a model for both a successful, relatively inexpensive program for the elderly, and a project that helps support dancers who are members of a professional company. This has not been an easy path to take. It is difficult in our culture for an artist to involve him- or herself in the community, even part time, and not lose some of the mythical status of artist. Part of the reason this is difficult is that artists themselves believe in the myth. For many in our culture, the artist is still viewed as an alienated, self-sacrificing, asocial being who depends on neurosis to produce great art. It is time for the myths to die, but the transition is difficult, since those artists who do involve themselves in the community are termed therapists, social workers, or at best arts workers. With the work of organizations such as the Dance Exchange, the boundaries of dance and art are stretched to include all people once again.

There is a growing movement of artists in this country who finds the most stimulating and challenging work to be in the community. By this, they mean a close encounter with their audience, often in a nontraditional performing space. Many are getting their creative material for songs, plays, and dances from the people they meet. The performance may be informal, but the contact is intense. The commitment to make art a meaningful experience for those who may never have been inside a traditional theater or concert hall is part of the motivation. For the dancer stepping into a senior center, the world opens to reveal myriad ways of discovering movement potential, wonderful personalities to copy in performance, and acceptance of one's performing skills. This generates exciting energy.

NEW DIRECTIONS

This work has discussed in some depth the involvement of artists with the community, but there is much to explore further. In fact, the successes of this program demonstrate that there is much more that could be done, developed, and researched to understand more fully the relations between art process, community organization, and the needs of special populations.

Training

Training is clearly needed. As this and other programs utilizing dance for older populations become known, more people will want to avail themselves of training opportunities.

Because of the nature of this work, training can take place in many different environments and can be geared to the needs of the people concerned. For example, I have been involved in workshops for dancers, health professionals, and recreation, physical, and arts therapists. Each of these groups can gain from understanding the use of dance with senior adults.

Training Dancers and Therapists

Dancers requesting information and training have been offered opportunities to assist the ongoing class at the Roosevelt. As other senior dance classes were developed, the training continued with on-site observation. Occasional sessions were held where all the senior adult dance teachers gathered and shared their experiences.

The Dance Exchange received requests for training workshops from organizations with concerns about dance for other special populations or from groups already doing recreational work with older people. In response to demand for further consultation, several eight-week seminars have been taught at the Roosevelt. These consisted of one-hour discussion and problem solving sessions followed by the ongoing Roosevelt dance class. During regular class time, seminar students taught different segments of the class while supervised by Dance Exchange teachers.

There are no formal evaluations of these sessions, but some comments from participants have indicated the effect this work has had on their thinking and feelings about dance and older people. "The class the other night was wonderful . . . I had no idea that they could move so beautifully and energetically," said one participant. Also from this class, a dance therapist commented, "This class offers me so much, the people are so open, and into their dancing. It is a revelation."

Similar sessions have been held in other cities in the United States and Canada. Comments from a recent gathering in Columbia, South Carolina, included this from the artistic director of the local modern dance company, who said, "A complete new world has opened up to me today. . . " (Evaluation form, South Carolina Arts Commission, 1981). An occupational therapist in the same group said, "I found this workshop stimulating to me. It can help me with a large variety of my patients." Many of the participants at this workshop were activity directors at senior citizen centers. One commented, "I enjoyed the program and found it stimulating and educational. I'd love to see more. Hope to get the seniors in my center dancing."

The material in this book can be adapted to different elderly populations, including stroke victims and other less active people. It could also be adapted to challenge the very active. In addition, with sensitive guidance, portions of this work could be adapted to other special populations such as handicapped children and the incarcerated. The chapter on improvisation could be especially useful.

Currently, training in the field is very generalized. Even this book considers the dancer and recreational therapist or activity director in the same breath, but care must be taken to address their individual skills and deficiencies. This is an important next step. The dancer might act as consultant, providing ex-

pertise and guidance as the program developed. It is assumed that the resources of the therapeutic community can be enriched by learning these dance
activities. The end product would be different from one based purely on artistic goals but still beneficial to the elderly.

Most important, at least as far as experience goes, is the potential for
dancers serving as consultants in the training of other professionals who will
work with the elderly. An example of this occurred when I spoke to a second-
year medical class at the University of Florida. The lecture consisted of class
participation in a typical senior adult warm-up series, stories designed to illustrate nonmedical solutions to health problems of the elderly, and a videotape
presentation of the Dancers of the Third Age. The major point stressed re-
peatedly was that the old are human beings, not medical and social problems.
Two of the medical students' remarks are reprinted here from the Dance Exchange files as evidence of the need for new levels of awareness in the medical
field.

> This was truly an enlightening experience. I discovered (1) she got me going, and (2)
> got me thinking — two things medical school has been rather deficient in.

> It is funny how we tend to shun older people because they are slow and senile and all
> those other peculiarities we attribute to the older people. I never realized just how
> much we, our culture as a whole, expect older people to fit into this mold, and with a
> little effort we can make such a difference by changing their images of themselves
> and, by doing so, change our images of them.

The Older Dancer as Teacher

The Dance Exchange program has kept its focus on the professional dancer
and his or her needs. This contributes to its success but something is missing.
While concentrating on training the younger dancer, the older dancer's potential was not fully developed. This is particularly true in teaching. Over the
years, the older students clearly gained enough skills to be able to assist and
teach. In fact, whenever a Dance Exchange teacher was unavailable, the seniors taught themselves, relying on the Dancers of the Third Age for leadership.
This independence is admirable and could be developed into a very interesting
program.

Having older people teaching younger students could increase intergenerational contact, and foster a deep sense of humanness. For the older person it
means self-worth and more reason to live. For the younger person it means a
relationship with someone who is experienced in life. In the late spring of 1981,
the Dance Exchange did a workshop in an elementary school in which the
Dancers of the Third Age taught the children a movement session. They still
needed the guidance of a professional dancer, but with training, they could easily run their own movement workshops.

RESEARCH

Performance versus Exercise

The physical and psychological benefits for the elderly begin almost immediately with the ongoing classes. However, for those in the group who choose to increase their commitment by performing on a semiregular basis, the benefits increase dramatically. These people experience an additional sense of self-satisfaction and self-worth as they master difficult material and stressful situations and develop strong personal relationships with younger people. It is suggested that research on all aspects of performance be done on a group of older people who have not had previous performance experience.

Effects on Arts Institutions

The involvement of a professional dance organization in the community requires resources, but it also allows for access to funding sources, community support, publicity, and a broad public base that most small arts organizations do not enjoy.

It is recommended that a research team study the economic impact of such work on arts organizations and on the communities they serve. If the evidence points in favor of increased community activity by professional organizations, perhaps this would be another incentive for providing these activities beyond the artistic ones cited in this book.

Positive results might also encourage local government, business, and civic groups to support the arts further.

Effects on Senior Center Institutions

As the gerontological community examines its priorities for spending, it is important that its members have a realistic and clear picture of the benefits of this kind of program. In addition to the individual growth of the older people who dance, it is the belief of this writer that the senior center itself gains from the presence of a modern dance class. There is a communal sense of vitality and joy that pervades the environment, affecting even those who walk by. For the staff, there is the opportunity to view the elderly in positive situations, contradicting for at least an hour their depression or isolation.

It is therefore recommended that a study be made of the overall benefits to an institution that sponsors this kind of activity. Finances, staffing needs, and safety should be measured against the positive effects of such a program to determine whether this work is valuable. In combination with the research observing the individual benefits accrued from dancing, these studies could be very persuasive tools for the establishment of more dance classes for the elderly.

Finale

Dance as an art form can bring to older people health, vitality, self-understanding, and a sense of belonging. Contact with the elderly can contribute to the artistic development of the younger dancer. A form of modern dance that incorporates structured warm-ups, improvisation, and performance challenges the senior adults to extend their movement range and communicative skills, while the teachers provide a safe environment through acceptance and support. The dancers, too, gain in the development of teaching and performing skills.

Written in 1978 by Jean Nordhaus for the *Washington Review of the Arts*, these paragraphs best describe, from an outsider's perspective, the power of this work.

> When Lerman first started teaching at the Roosevelt Hotel in spring 1975, there were only 12 tentative participants, with a scattering of others looking on. But the night I saw the class, the ballroom in the old hotel was filled, and most of the "onlookers" sitting along the side lines in chairs and wheel chairs were participating to whatever extent they were able.
>
> We are so accustomed to thinking of dance in connection with youth and of old age in terms of restriction of movement and energy, that watching older people dancing is a startling experience at first. And when, after elaborate warm ups and much cajoling and good-humored bullying from Lerman, quite a few of her senior students, using the backs of their chairs as barres, dared a jump, those small triumps in the on-going battle with gravity were as beautiful, on their own terms, as one of Baryshnikov's double cabrioles.[1]

The dancer, whether young or old, experiences the world through his or her art. He or she is concerned with craft, content, form, and communication. The craft is built through physical training; the content, through observation; the form, through aesthetic decision making; and the communication, through a combination of skill, desire, and commitment to the belief in the validity of the performance process. These experiences are of value to human beings. Although people may not ultimately become dancers or perceive of themselves as dancers, they can have a vital life experience through this connection to an art form. For most participants at the Roosevelt, art is probably not uppermost in their minds, but it is through the art experience that the rest is taking place.

---

[1]From Jean Nordhaus, "Liz Lerman — Dance and Life and Death," the *Washington Review of the Arts*, 1978, p. 3.

Figure 89. John Johnson and Liz Lerman.
PHOTO: Anonymous

BIBLIOGRAPHY

Achenbaum, W. *Old Age in the New Land.* Baltimore: Johns Hopkins University Press, 1978.

Billig, N. Evaluating the Effects of a Therapeutic/Recreational Dance Class on Elderly Participants, A Research Proposal. (dissertation, Catholic University of America, 1980.)

Browne, G. Ms. Galaxy and Her Three Raps with God. *The Columbia Flier,* June 23, 1977, p. 30.

Burnside, M., ed. *Working with the Elderly: Group Process and Techniques.* North Scituate, Mass.: Duxbury Press, 1976.

Butler, R. *Why Survive?* New York: Harper & Row, 1975.

Caplow-Linder, E., Harpaz, L., and Samberg, S. *Therapeutic Dance/Movement: Expressive Activities for Older Adults.* New York: Human Science Press, 1979.

Dance Exchange. Evaluation of Workshops (files). Washington, D.C., 1976-1981.

— — —. Love Letters from Kids (files). Washington, D.C., 1976-1981.

— — —. Support Letters on Performance (files). Washington, D.C., 1976-1981.

Davis, D. *Artculture, Essays on the Post Modern.* New York: Harper & Row, 1977.

Ellfeldt, L. *Dance from Magic to Art.* Dubuque, Iowa: Wm. C. Brown Company, 1976.

Faske, I. Elderly Group — Wonderful Troupe. *The Hatchet,* March 2, 1978, p. 10.

Fishman, L. Interviews with Dancers of the Third Age. Washington, D.C., 1979.

Hanna, J. L. *To Dance is Human: A Theory of Nonverbal Communication.* Austin: University of Texas Press, 1979.

H'Doubler, M.A. *Dance as a Creative Art Experience.* New York: Appleton-Century-Crofts, 1940.

Hennessy, M. J. Music and Group Work with Aged. *Nursing and the Aged.* Edited by I. Burnside. New York: McGraw-Hill, 1976.

Kriegsman, A. Liz Lerman. *The Washington Post,* April 14, 1978, p. B6.

Krucoff, C. Senior Citizens Say Dancing Puts Them "On Top of the World." *The Washington Post,* May 26, 1977, p. DC4.

Lerman, L. Personal notebooks. Washington, D.C., 1974-1981.

National Association for Human Development. *Moderate Exercise for People Over Sixty.* Washington, D.C., 1977.

National Council on the Aging. *The Arts, the Humanities and Older Americans: A Catalogue of Program Profiles.* Washington, D.C.: National Council on the Aging, 1981.

Nisbet, R. *The Quest for Community.* London: Oxford University Press, 1953.

Nordhaus, J. Liz Lerman — Dance and Life and Death. *The Washington Review of the Arts,* 1978, p. 3.

Plutchik, R., Conte, H.R., Weiner, M.B., and Teresi, J. Studies of Body Image, IV: Drawing in Normal and Abnormal Geriatric and Non-Geriatric Groups. *Journal of Gerontology,* *33*:68-75, 1978.

Sakon, S., and Elton, M. *Physical Change and Aging: A Guide for the Helping Professions.* New York: Tiresias Press, 1978.

Shepard, R. *Physical Activity and Aging.* Chicago: Year Book Medical Publishers, 1978.

Smith, G. *Care of the Patient with a Stroke.* New York: Springer Publishing Company, 1976.

Spolin, V. *Improvisation for the Theater.* Chicago: Northwestern University Press, 1963.

Weiber, P., and Rathbone, E. *Adult Day Care: Community Work with the Elderly.* New York: Springer Publishing Company, 1978.

Wilding-White, A. Ordinary People. *The Washington Tribune,* May 22-June 4, 1981, p. 16.

Woodruff, D., and Birren, J. *Aging: Scientific Perspective and Social Issues.* London: D. Van Nostrand Company, 1975.

INDEX

The reference "figs. 45-47" is to the figures on pp. 45-47. When both text and figures on a page pertain to a topic, a page number only is given.

A

Abdomen, 22

Ability (*see* Capabilities)

Acceptance of dancers by teacher, classmates, or audiences, 6-7, 66, 106-107, 144, 150, 154

Accidents, 19, 95

Accompaniment, musical (*see* Musical accompaniment)

Activity centers, 11 (*see also* Senior centers)

Activity directors. xv, xvi, 10, 18, 151

Actors, 123

Adams, Don, xx

Administration of dance classes, svi, 10-19

Administrators, xv, xvi, 9, 14, 17-18

Admission fees, 9, 134

Adults, senior (*see* Senior adults)

Air texture (theme), 113

Alienation (*see* Isolation)

Alzheimer's groups, 12

Ambulatory persons (*see* Moving)

American Association of Retired Persons, The, xvii

Anger, expression of, 56, 99

Animals (images), 125

Ankle joints,75

Ankles, crossing of, 6, fig. 67

Apartments, independent, 11

Arabesque (exercise), 88-90

Arguments among students, 13, 106

Arm circle (exercise), 43-49

Arms, 15, 16, 103, 114, 141
   circling of, 43, figs. 44-40, 78, figs. 79-80
   crossing and opening of, 66, figs. 70-71,
   fig. 80, 121
   crossing of body with, 78, figs. 79-80
   improvisations with, 43-44, 60
   natural movements of, 44
   reaching with, 39, figs. 40-42, 43, figs. 44-49, 53, figs. 54-55, fig. 59, 78, 88
   stretching of, 21

Art
   definition of, 8, 119, 137
   therapy as, 5, 150-151

Art galleries (theme), 135

Arthritis, s141

Artists, 123

Arts organizations, 18, 149, 150, 153

Arts programs, 12, 148, 149-150, 153

Assistants at dance classes, 20, 74-75, 88, 93, 94, 98, 119, 121

Audience participation dances, 125, 126, 128-129, 152

Audiences, 4, 8, 9, 106, 125, 127, 133-134, 144, 148, 150
   (*see also* Children in audiences and Observers)

B

Back, 93

Balance, 88, 97-98, 142, 144

Ballet, 3, 75

Ballet positions, 74, (*see also* specific positions)

Ballet steps, xii, 75-76, 81, 85, 88

Ballin' the Jack (dance), 128, 132

Baltimore, (Mdl), 142

Barres, 74, 154

Baryshnikov, Mikhail, 154

Beach (theme), 108

159

Bear and mailman (story), 125-126
Beauty
  dance, in, xii, 6, 8, 95, 112, 151, 154
  senior adults, of, 6
Beds, dancing by persons in, 103
Belanger, Harry, xx, 124, 136, 140, 142, 143, 149
Belin, Marty, xix, fig. 133
Belly, 22, 103
Belongings, personal, 20
Bend and rise (exercise), 75-76, fig. 77, 91
Bernstein, Diane, xix
Birds (images), 106, 114
Birthday parties (theme), 108
Bliss, Jeff, xix
Boats (theme), 110
Body, xii, xiii, 4, 21, 104-105
  images of the, 6, 17, 74
  weight of the, 22
Body types, xi, 145
Bonsai (dance), fig. 138, 149
Boredom, expression of, fig. 108
Breathing, 22, fig. 23
Breathing (exercise), 22-23
Breen, James, xix
Browne, Ginna, 136, 157
Buckley, Mary, xix

C

Calisthenics (theme), 113
Capabilities of dancers, xi, 21, 60, 144-145, 149, 150, 154
  differences among, 66, 94, 144, 152
  technical, 7, 117, 126, 154
Caplowe, Debra, xix
Cat (image), 125, fig. 126
Cement (image), 99
Chairs, xvi, 11, 21, 73, 94, 117, 154, (*see also* Exercises: sitting and Sitting)
  dances while sitting in, 103, 107-108, figs. 109-111, 114, 118, 121
  positioning of, 15, 43
  props for exercises, as, 39, 50, 74-75, 76, fig. 77, 78, 81, 85, fig. 86, 88, figs. 89-90, 91, fig. 92, 93, 99
Challenges, 4, 73, 95, 105, 120, 145, 153, 154 (*see also* Exercises: difficult)
Chanukah (theme), 109
Charisma, 18
Children in audiences, 125, 126-127, 133, 142, 152
Children's Hospital, National Medical Center, xvii
Choreographers, 4, 8, 139, 140, 145-146
Christmas (theme), 109

Chronic ailments, 10
Churches, 11
Circles of dancers, 15, 21, 96, 98, 118, 120, 121
Clapping, 43, 53, fig. 55, 66, fig. 72, 102
Clothes, 9, 16-17 (*see also* Costumes)
Clouds (image), 106
Coaching, 7, 110, 114
Cohn, Alix, xix
Cole, Nancy, xix
Collisions among dancers, 78, 85, 102
Columbia Flier, 136, 157
Colors (themes), 113
Columbia (S.C.), 151
Combinations of movements, 30, 43, 60-72
Communication (*see* Expression in dance)
Community, xi, xii-xiii, 127, 142, 147-148, 150, 153, 154
  dance, 75, 140, 147, 153
Competitiveness, 119, 126, 144
Complexity of movements, 44, 66, 81
Concerts, xv, 9, 119, 134-138
  scheduling of, 9
  (*see also* Performances: formal)
Confidence, 4, 7, 116
Confusion, 66, 78
Consultants, 10, 152
Conversations, 13, 56, 106, 117, 121, 122, 137
Costumes, 134 (*see also* Clothes)
Crippled persons, 6, 141
Criticism
  dance students, of, 7, 106-107
  dancers, of, 135-137, 144
Cunningham, Merce, 8

D

Dance
  benefits of, xi, xvi, 3-5, 7, 139-148, 153, 154
  definitions of terms for, 6-9
  ethnic, 3
  interpretive, 3
  modern, xvi, 3-5, 8, 128, 154
  styles of, 3-4, 14, 128 (*see also* Dance forms; Disco; Folk dances; Folk forms; Freestyle dancing; Marches; Rock 'n roll; "Show biz" dance style; Waltzes)
  therapy, as, 5, 150-151
  traditions of, 4, 7, 8, 74, 76, 88, 121
Dance classes
  administration of, xvi, 10-19
  assistants at (*see* Assistants at dance classes)
  attendance at, 17
  definition of, 8
  demonstration of (*see* Demonstrations: public)
  disruptions at, 13, 96, 145

funding of, 18, 147, 149-150, 153
location of, 12, 15
recruitment for, 17
scheduling of, 12, 17, 18, 96, 116
seating at, 15-16
size of, 14
structure in, 22, 120, 124
theory of, xvi, 5, 6-9, 21-21
Dance community, 75, 140, 147, 153
Dance Exchange, xv, xvii, 16, 19, 95, 114, 124, fig. 133, 134, 139, 140, 147, 148, 150, 151, 152
Dance Exchange Performance Company, xv, 124, 135, 136
Dance forms, 3-4 (*see also* Dance: styles of)
Dance from Magic to Art (Ellfeldt), 4, 157
Dance programs, 9, 10-19, 143, 153-154
Dance teachers, 5, 14, 18, 122, 140, 147, 148, 154
    training of, 150-153
Dancers, 8, 144
    amateur, 4, 154
    older, 124, 126, 134, 135-137, 139-143, 144, 145-148, 149, 151
    professional, xi, xii-xiii, xv, xvi, 9, 10, 123, 133, 143-148, 149-150, 152-153
    younger, 126, 129, 134, 136, 139-140, 143-148, 154
Dancers of the Third Age, xv, 16, 123-138, 143, 152
Day Care facilities, 11-12
Dean, Sarah, xix
Death, xi, 124
Death (theme), 111-112
DeLoria, Dennis, xix
Demonstration(s), 15, 21, 30, 44, 50, fig. 522, 66, 74-75, 85, 91, 96, 101
    public, 123-124
Desert (theme), 113
Dewey, John, 5
Disasters (theme), 110
Disco, 3, 14
Disruptions at dance classes, 13, 96, 145
District of Columbia Commission on the Arts and Humanities, xix
Dizziness, 50, 93, 97
Donations, 18
Dreaming (theme), 113
Drummers, 14-15
Duets (*see* Partnering)
Duncan, Isadora, 5
Dunn, Carol, xix
Dynamics, 24, 39, 56, 99, 144

E

Ears, 24
Eating (theme), 109-110, 113, 118

Education by dance, 124, 142, 148, 152
Eidenberg, Susan, xvii
Elbows
    bending of, 93
    circling of, 22, 33, fig. 34
Elevator Operators and Other Strangers (dance), 136-149
Ellfeldt, Lois, 4, 157
Embarrassment, 14, 15, 16, 17-18, 22, 78, 94, 98
    expression of, 111
Embodiment, 104-107
Emergencies, 19
Emotion (*see* Feelings and Moods)
Endurance, 102, 116, 141, 144
Energy in dance (*see* Force of movements)
Enthusiasm, 17, 39
Environments (themes), 98, 99, 106, 113-114
Esthetics in dance, 117, 143, 145-146, 152, 154
Everyday activities (themes), 98, 112-113
Excitement, 85, 102, 117, 124, 126-127, 135, 145, 149, 150
    expression of, 107, fig. 110
Exercise, 3, 16, 17, 123, 125, 153
    dance as, xi, xvi, xv, 16
Exercises (*see also* Warm-ups)
    difficult, 53, 66, 76, 88, 120, 125 (*see also* Challenges)
    sitting, xvi, 22-73, 76, 81, 94 (*see also* Chairs and Sitting)
    standing, xvi, 74-93
Expansion Arts Program (National Endowment for the Arts), xvii
Expression
    dance, in, 124, 126, 127, 145, 146, 148, 154
    freedom of, 4, 105
Eye contact, 21
Eyes, 24, 50, 78

F

Face, improvisation with, 103
Falling leaves (image), 113
Falls, 74, 95, 97, 125, 142
Fatigue, 33, 57, 58, 116, 135, (*see also* Resting)
    expression of, 107
Fear, 97, 119
    expression of, 126
Feelings, xii, 3, 4, 5, 7, 17, 96, 108, 121, (*see also* Moods)
Feelings (themes), 98, 107-108, figs. 109-110, 111-112, 113 (*see also* Anger; Boredom; Embarrassment; Excitement; Fatigue; Fear; Friendliness; Independence; Joy; Pride; Sadness)
Feet, 57, 58, 76, 78, 103, 141 (*see also* Foot combination I; Foot combination II; Foot tap)
    brushing of, on floor, 60, figs. 64-65, 81

crossing and opening of, 66, figs. 67-68, figs. 70-71

raising and lowering of, 60, figs. 62-65, 75, fig. 77

shuffling of, 60, 64-65

tapping of, 81, figs. 82-84

turning out of, 75, 85, 88

Feet I (exercise), 60-63

Feet II: brush (exercise), 60, 64-65

Feet III: crossings (exercise), 66-68

Feet IV: practice jump (sitting exercise), 66, 69

Fingers, 43, 103

stretching of, 35, figs. 36-38

Fingers (exercise), 35-38

Finkelstein, Rebecca, xx

Fireworks (image), 109

Fish (image), 114, fig. 115

Fist making, 35-38, 39, 56

Flashenberg, Liesel, xix

Flautists, 14-15

Flower (image), 35

Floyd, Diane, xix

Fog (image), 99

Fogelgren, Bob, xix, 145

Folk forms, 116, 121, fig. 122

Folk dances, 14

Follow the leader (technique), 98, 99, 114, 117

Food (theme), 109-110, 113, 118

Foot combination I: soft shoe (exercise), 60-65

Foot combination II (exercise), 66-72

Foot tap (exercise), 81-84

Force of movements, 24, 39, 56, 99, 144

Forest (image), 125

Forgetfulness, 6

Form, 6, 7, 154

Forward spine curve (sitting exercise), 50-52

Forward spine curve (standing exercise), 93

Foster Grandparents, 133

Fourth of July (theme), 109, 118-119.

Free-style dancing, 100, 101, 102, fig. 103, 106

Freedom (theme), 109, 118

Freezing cold (image), 100

Friendliness, expression of, 103

Frustration, 7, 88, 95

Fun, xi, 8, 17, 60, 95, 96, 97, 103, 106, 108, 125, 133-134, 139, 141

Funding of dance classes, 18, 147, 149-150, 153

G

Ganshauer, Diane Hull, xix

Gardening (theme), 113

George Washington University, xvii, 134

Germany, 147

Gold (image), 128-129

Goldbard, Arlene, xx

Goodman, Keith, xix

Government subsidies, 18

Graham, Martha, 8, 147

Grants, 18, 150

Gray Panthers, 133

Great Depression, 147

Greetings, 20

Group activities, xi, 5, 95, 96

Group discussions, 13, 15

Guitarists, 14-15

H

Hallenbeck, Vee, xx, fig. 106, fig. 120, fig. 122, 124, 125, figs. 132-133, fig. 138, 141, 149

Halloween (theme), 109, 113

Hand/arm reach (exercise), 39-42, 43

Hand holding, 15, 96, 97-98, 103, 120, 121

Handicapped persons, 142, 151

Hands

clapping of (*see* clapping)

improvisation with, 60, 103, 111

opening and closing of, 35, figs. 36-38

placement of, on chairs, 74, 75, fig. 77, 78, 88, figs. 89-90, 91, fig. 92, 93

placement of, on shoulders, 22, 33

punching with, 56

reaching with, 39, figs. 40-42, 43, figs. 44-49, 53, figs. 54-55

Harris, Betty, xx, 125, fig. 132, fig. 133

Haskins, Louise, xx

The Hatchet (George Washington University), 134

Hawk (image), 125

Hayes, Patrick, xix

Head

circling of, 28, fig. 29, 120

lowering and raising of, 50, figs. 51-52, 75, 78, 93

rocking of, 73

stretching of, 24, figs. 25-27, 53, figs. 54-55

Head (exercise), 24-27

Head/torso (exercise), 28-29

Health

mental, 3, 5, 19, 139, 142, 153, 154

physical, 3, 19, 94, 108, 124, 139, 141-142, 153, 154

Health professionals, 150-151, 152

Hearing, 21, 145

Heels

standing with, together, 85

touching of, to floor, 60, fig. 63, 75

Hip joints, 22, 75

Hips, 103

Holidays (themes), 43, 98, 109-110, 113, 118-

119 (*see also* Chanukah; Christmas; Fourth of July; Halloween; Passover; Thanksgiving)

Hospitals, xv, 10, 11, 12

Human potential, xi, 5, 6-7, 124

Humanitarianism, 142, 147, 152

Humor, 13, 16, 22, 24, 30, 56, 66, 78, 102, 103, 111, 126, 127, 133-134

I

Ideas, xii, xvi, 5, 8, 44, 96, 99-100, 107, 112, 114, 117, 148, 154 (*see also* Themes)

Images (themes), 98, 114, fig. 115, 119, 145 (*see also* Animals; Birds; Cat; Cement; Clouds; Falling leaves; Fireworks; Fish; Fog; Forest; Freezing cold; Gold; Hawk; Kite; Mushroom; Nature; Rainbow; Scaring pigeons; Snow; Squirrel; Stars; Swans; Taffy; Trees; Wheat; Wind)

Imagination, 4, 13, 95, 105, 139, 148

Impairments, 10, 140

Improvisation, xii, xvi, xv, 3, 4, 9, 17, 119, 123, 125, 126, 143, 148, 154

  definition of, 8, 117

  chairs, without, 94-115, 116

  material for, 98, 108-115

  musical accompaniment of, 15, 98

  sitting, while, 43-44, 60, 94

  structures in, 95, 96-97, 98, 100, 103, 107, 110, 114, 115, 117

  techniques for, list 98, 99-108

  theory of, 95-96

Quest for Community, The, (Nisbet), 148, 157

Independence, expression of, 118, 119

Independent apartments, 11

Individual progress, 14, 96

Individual students, helping of, 75, 122

Informal performances (*see* Performances, informal)

Insurance, 19

Intellectual stimulation, xi, 5

Intergenerational performances, 142, 144, 149 (*see also* Dance Exchange Performance Company, Dancers of the Third Age)

Intergenerational relationships, xi, xv, 6, 101, 119, 133-134, 137, 139-148, 153

Introductions

  performances, of, 124-125

  solo dances, as, 96-98, 119, 124, 142

Isolation, xiii, 5, 109, 148, 153

Isolations (exercise movements), 30, 35

J

Jacobson, Solomon, xx

Japan, 147

Johnson, John, xx, 124, 125, 141, fig. 155

Johnson, Nancy, xix, xx

Joints, 21-22, 75

Jourdin, Judith, xx, fig. 105, fig. 120, fig. 122, fig. 132, 149

Joy, xii, xiii, 16, 60, 97, 124, 140, 146, 148, 153

  expression of, 95, 107, 111

Jumping, 91, fig. 92, 154

  sitting, while, 66, fig. 69, fig. 72

Jumps (standing exercise), 91-92

Jungle (theme), 113, 114

K

Karate movements, 125

Kinesthetic sensations, 33, 50

Kite (image), 104-107

Knee lift (exercise), 57, 58, 85-87

Knees

  bending of, 75-76, 78, 91

  lifting of, 22, 57, 58, fig. 59, 85, figs. 86-87, 120

Knowledge, sharing of, xiii

Kramer, Arnold, xx

Kennedy Center, 134

Kriegsman, Alan, 136, 157

Krucoff, Carol, 141, 157

L

Lamb, Deborah, xx

Laughter (*see* Humor)

Leadership by teacher, 110, 114

Leaning, 78

Legal, Lee, xx, 125

Legs, 76, 91, 103

  circling of, 43

  lifting of, 57, 66, 69, 88, fig. 90

  shifting weight to, 78

  stretching of, 58, fig. 59, 85, fig. 87

Lerman, Liz, fig. 52, fig. 120, fig. 122, fig. 132, fig. 135, 136, 154, fig. 155

Life, xi, xii, 140, 152, 154

Life experiences of senior adults (*see* Senior adults: life experiences of and Memories of dancers)

Lighting, 9, 119, 134

Limón, José, 8

Location of dance classes, 12, 15

Long-term care facilities, 10

Loosening up, 8, 141, 143,

Lunges (exercise), 78

M

MacDonald, Ann, xix

McClain, Ron, xix

McKelvey, Janice, xix
Mailman and bear (story), 125-126
Marches, 14
Material for dances (*see* Ideas; Improvisation: material for; Themes)
Mayo, Lenore, xx
Maxwell, Elliot, xix
Media, mixed, 114
Medical checkups, 19
Medical consent forms, 19
Memories of audience, 137
Memories of dancers, 17, 108-109, (*see also* Senior adults: life experiences of)
Memories (themes), 98, 108-109, 118
Memorization of dances, 95, 118, 120
Memorization of names, 96
Mental health (*see* Health: mental)
Michigan, 125
Millen, Joan, xix
Mind, xii, 4, 105
Mirroring, 15, 78, 85
Mirroring (technique), 98, 100-101, fig. 102, 115, 126
Mistakes, 9, 14, 30, 50, 52, 78, 95, 126
Modern dance (*see* Dance: modern)
Moods, 95, 99, 113, 114 (*see also* Feelings)
Motivation, 14, 16, 21, 94, 97, 117-118, 124
Mountains (theme), 108
Movement, 4, 6-7, 14, 150 (*see also* Pure movement)
Movement vocabularies, 4, 8
Movements
  adaptations of, 7, 16, 76, 81, 94, 101, 121, 151
  combinations of, 30, 43, 60-72
  complexity of, 44, 66, 81
  force of, 24, 39, 56, 99, 144
  free-style, 100, 101, 102, fig. 103, 106
  range of, 39, 66, 154
  repetitions of, 21, 22, 57, 99-100, 121
  structures of (*see* Scripts and Structures in movements)
  unison, 119
Movie stars (themes), 109
Moving, xii, 11, 20, 75, 141, 146
Ms. Galaxy and her Three Raps with God (dance), 136, 137
Mushroom (image), 125
Music, 12, 13, 14-15, 95, 114
Musical accompaniment, xvi, 10-11, 14-15, 60, 81, 98, 99, 101, 102, 118
Musicians, 14-15
Mylecraine, Mary, xx, 142, 143

N

NCAH (*see* National Committee for Arts and the Handicapped)

Nachtigal, Daniel, xix
Names (themes), 97
Nash, Sally, xx
National Committee for Arts and the Handicapped (NCAH), 133, 134
National Council on the Aging, xix, 133
National Endowment for the Arts, xvii, 18
Nature (images), 114, fig. 115
Neck, curving of, 50-52
New Horizons (program, Chidren's Hospital), xvii
Nisbet, Robert, 148, 157
Noise, 12, 13
Nordhaus, Jean, 154, 157
Notebooks, 19, 146
Novelty, 140
Nurses, xvi
Nursing homes, 10, 143
Nutrition sites, 9, 11, 12

O

Observers, 8, 12, 13, 17, 94, 96, 151, 153, 154 (*see also* Audiences)
Occupational therapists, 151
Office buildings, xv
Olhofsky, Olena, xx, 124
O'Neill Theater Center Choreographer's Conference, 135
Overachievers, 21, 33, 73, 119

P

Pain, 19, 21, 22, 39, 122
Park (theme), 95
Partnering, 93, 97, 99, 100-101, 121
Passé (exercise), 85-87
Passés, 85, fig. 86, 120
Passover (theme), 109
Patterson, Jim, xix
Pearson, Mary Francis, xix
Pendleton, Elisabeth, xx
Performances, xvi, 16, 123-138, 140, 147, 153, 154
  dance as, xii-xiii
  definition of, 8-9
  formal, xv, 4, 9, 119, 129, 134-138, 143 (*see also* Concerts)
  informal, xii, 4, 9, 96, 116, 117-119, 123-134, 150
  intergenerational, 142, 144, 149 (*see also* Dancers of the Third Age and Dance Exchange Performance Company)
Peripheral actions, 22
Phrase building (technique), 98, 99, 112, 117, 118
Phrases in dances, 43-49, 66-72, 116, 120, 125
Physical limitations, 4, 19, 94, 101, 140, 141-

142, 151-152, 154
Physical therapists, 151
Pianists, 14-15
Picnic (theme), 118
Plays, 150
Plié and relevé (exercise), 75-77
Pliés, 7, 75-76, 78, 91
Poetry (themes), 98, 114
Poets, 123
Popular music, 14
Powell, Edward, xx, fig. 132
Prejudice, 96
Press, 9, 136-137
Pride, expression of, 99, fig. 111
Prisoners, 151
Privacy, 12, 14, 121
Progress of dance students, 14, 96, 117, 121, 144
Prosterman, Bea, xix
Public space, 12
Publicity, 16, 153
Punch (exercise), 56-57
Punching, 56
Pure movement (themes), 98, 114-115
Push-ups, 93, 134

R

Race, 96
Rainbow, The, (dance), 128-129, 132
Rainbows (images), 128
Ramsey, Martha, xix
Range of movements, 39, 66, 154
Rea, Helen, xix, figs. 132-133, 136, 144, 149
Rea, Jess, xx, fig. 92, 107, fig. 120, fig. 122, 125, fig. 132, 149
Record keeping, 18-19
Recreational therapists, xv, xvi, 151
Recreational programs, 12, 151
Rehearsals, 9, 14, 117, 124-125, 133, 134, fig. 135, 137
Relaxation, xvi, 28, 78, 141
Relevé (*see* Plié and relevé)
Reminders, 16, 21, 75
Repertory pieces, 4, 135
Repetitions of movements, 21, 22, 57, 99-100, 121
Research needs, xvi, 153-155
Residences, 10-11
Resting, 13, 30, 58, 95, 117, 141 (*see also* Fatigue)
Reticence, 117-118
Retirement villages, 11
Reuther, Sophie, xix
Rhythm, 85, 95, 99-100, 102
Right and left, 15-16, 78
Right and wrong (*see* Mistakes)
Rock 'n roll, 128
Rocking of body, 73

Roosevelt for Senior Citizens, The, xi, xv, xix, 11, 12, 13, 14, 15, 16, 95, 96, fig. 103, 107, 109, 114, 118, 120, 123, 136, 141, 143, 146, 151, 154
Rote learning, 75
Rothenberg, Betty, xx
Rother, Charles, xx
Routines (*see* Exercises; Structure in dance clases; Structures in movements)
Russia, 125

S

Sadness, expression of, fig. 109, 111
Safety, 7, 74-75, 88, 91, 93, 95, 97, 144, 153, 154
Sarvis, Paul, 135
Satisfaction, personal, 5, 101, 139-148, 153
Scaring pigeons (image), 113
Scheduling of concerts, 9
Scheduling of dance classes, 12, 17, 18, 96, 116
Schools, xv, 9, 126-127, 134, 152
Schreiber, Elsie, fig. 103
Scoliosis, 141
Scripts, 8, 145 (*see also* Structures in movements)
Sculptures (technique), 97, 98, 101-102, 115, 117, 118, 126
Seasons (themes), 98, 113
Security, 22, 74, 75, 145
Sedentary state, 116
Self-esteem, 116, 139, 140, 147, 152, 153
Self-expression
  dance as, xi, 143
  improvisation, through, 95, 105
Self-reliance, 18, 73, 74, 97, 144, 152
Self-understanding, 4, 5, 152, 154
Seminars, 151
Senility, 6, 152
Senior adults
  audiences, in, 142, 144, 148
  dancers, as (*see* Dancers: older)
  institutionalized, 5
  life experiences of, xii, 112, 125-126, 140, 146, 147, 148, 152, 154 (*see also* Memories of dancers)
  stereotypes of (*see* Stereotypes)
Senior centers, xv, 6, 7, 9, 10-12, 119, 123, 146, 150, 151, 153
  residential, 10-11, 143
  nonresidential, 11-12, (*see also* Activity centers)
Sequences, xii
Shadowing by teacher, 97
Shellow, Jill, xix
Shoes, 16-17
Shoulder circles (exercise), 33-34
Shoulder joints, circling of, 21
Shoulder lift (exercise), 30-32
Shoulders, 21-22, 24

circling of, 33, fig. 34
lifting of, 30, figs. 31-32
"Show biz" dance style, 128
Shuffle step, 60
Side-to-side shifts (exercise), 78
Sit bones, 28
Sitting, 15, 116, (*see also* Chairs)
Sitting exercises, xvi, 22-73, 76, 81, 94
Six-count torso (exercise), 53-55
Slavery (theme), 109
Sleeping or waking (theme), 113, 118
Snow (image), 113
Social centers, 11
Social self, 3
Social workers, 150
Soft shoe dancing, 60-65
Solo activities, 5, 95, 96, 98, 103
Songs, 118, 128, 150
Sounds (themes), 113, 118
South Carolina Art Commission, 151
Space, variations in, 99-100, 101
Speaking by dancers while moving, 81, 95, 96-97, 99, 124
Spelman, Jon, xvii
Spinning, 97
Special Constituencies Program (D.C. Commission on the Arts and Humanities), xvii
Spine, curving of, 50, figs. 51-52, 93
Spiritual self, 3
Spiritual uplift, xi
Spontaneity, 8, 119
Sports (theme), 126
Square dance, 121
Squirrel (image), 125
Staff
   attitudes of, 12-13
   participants, as, 17, 98
Staging, 9
Stamina, 102, 116, 141, 144
Standing, 73, 89, 116-122
Standing exercises, xvi, 74-93
Standing up (exercise), 73
Stars (images), 128
Stephansky, Kate, xix
Stereotypes, 6, 7, 128
   overcoming of, 124, 148, 151, 153, 154
Stomach, 22
Stories (themes), 98, 109, 110, 125-126, 146, 148
Strength, 22, 97-98, 102, 117, 121, 141
Stroke, 141, 151
Structure in dance classes, 22, 120, 124
Structures in movements, xii, 8, 43-44, 95, 96-97, 98, 100, 103, 107, 110, 114, 115, 116, 117, 121, 126. (*see also* Scripts)
Sunderland, Jackie, xix
Support, mutual, 6

Support of dancing seniors, physical, 75, 93, 94, 97, 154
Swan Lake (dance), 120, 141
Swans (image), 120
Swimming (theme), 113
Synagogues, 11

T

TV, 3, 14, 147
Taffy (image), 75
T'ai Chi, 114, 141
Teacher training residencies, xv
Techniques, xii, xiii, 3, 4, 126, 134, 137, 144, 147
   be an environment, 98, 103, 106
   be a person with the word, 98, 104-105
   build a phrase, 98, 99, 112, 117, 118
   follow the leader, 98, 99, 114, 117
   how would you be if, 98, 107-108, figs. 109-11
   isolations, 98, 99, 102-103
   list of, 98, 99-108
   mirroring, 98, 100-101, fig. 102, 115, 126
   pass the dance around, 98, 103
   sculptures, 97, 98, 101-102, 115, 117, 118, 126
   theme and variations, 43, 98, 99-100, 108, 112, 115
   word dances, 98, 103-107, 110, 113, 114, 117, 119, 126
Tempo, 57, 85, 95, 99, 125, 142
Tendu (exercise), 81-84, 88
Terrace Theater, Kennedy Center, 134
Thanksgiving (theme), 113
Theme and variations (technique), 43, 98, 99-100, 108, 112, 115
Themes, 14, 98, 108-115, 119, 122 (*see also* Air texture; Beach; Birthday party; Boats; Calisthenics; Colors; Death; Desert; Dreaming; Environments; Everyday activities; Feelings; Food; Freedom; Gardening; Holidays; Ideas; Images; Jungle; Mountains; Movie stars; Names; Park; Picnic; Poetry; Pure movement; Seasons; Slavery; Sleeping or waking; Sounds; Stories; Swimming; Theme and variations; Visiting with a friend; Walking to the store; Wood chopping)
Therapeutic programs, 12, 150-151, 152
Therapists (*see* Occupational therapists; Physical therapists; Recreational therapists)
Therapy art as, 5, 150-151
Thighs, 57, 73
Timing in dance (*see* Rhythm and Tempo)
Toes
   circling of, 58-59
   stretching of, 85, fig. 87
   touching of, to floor, 60, fig. 62, 88
   touching of, to knee, 85, 120

Torso, 56
  circling of, 28, fig. 29, 43
  rocking of, 57, 73, 88
  stretching of, 21, 53, figs. 54-55
Touching, 11, 21, 50, 101, 102
Transformations (dance), 127-131
Trees (images), 100, 106
Tulane, Thelma, xx, fig. 23, figs. 31-34, figs. 44-49, fig. 51, figs. 57-59, figs. 61-65, figs. 82-84, figs. 86-90, fig. 93, figs. 100-102, fig. 1-4, figs. 108-111, fig. 113, fig. 115, fig. 120, fig. 122, 124, 125, figs. 127-133, fig. 135, fig. 138, 140, 142, 143, 149
Twisting, 78, figs. 79-80
Twists (exercise), 78-80

U

U.S. Department of Health and Human Services, 18
U.S. Department of Housing and Urban Development, 18
Unison movements, 119
University of Florida, 152

V

Valenti, Bette, 134
Variations of themes (*see* Theme and variations)
Vaznaugh, Delfa, xx
Virginia Reel (dance), 121
Virtuosity, xii, xiii, 7
Visiting with a friend (theme), 113
Visitors, 12, 98
Vocabularies, 4, 8
Volunteers, 18

W

Walkers, 97, 116

Walking to the store (theme), 113
Waltzes, 14, 97
Warm-ups, xii, xvi, 15, 20-73, 125, 152, 154 (*see also* Exercises)
Washington (D.C.), xi, xvii, xviii, 11, 137
Washington Performing Arts Society, xvii
Washington Post, 136, 157
Washington Review of the Arts, 154
Waskow, Arthur, xx
Waxter Center (Baltimore), 142
Welch, Ada, xx, figs. 25-29, figs. 35-42, figs. 44-49, figs. 53-56, figs. 67-72, fig. 77, figs. 79-80, figs. 100-103, figs. 108-112, fig. 115, figs. 126-131, 142
Wells, Anna Mary, xx, 132
Wheelchairs, 58, 97, 103, 116, 141, 142, 154
Wheat (image), 78
Wheeler, Douglas, xix
Who's on First (dance), 126
Wind (image), 100, 106
Wolf Trap Foundation, xix
Wolff, Rima, xix, 114
Woman of the Clear Vision (dance), xi, 111, fig. 146, 149
Wood chopping (theme), 113, 125
Word dances (technique), 98, 103-107, 110, 113, 114, 117, 119, 126
Workshops, xv, 142, 150-151, 152

Y

Yglesias, Colette, 136

Z

Zuckerman, Don, xix, 125, 126, fig. 132, 144, 145, 147